THE FRAGILE BACHELOR

THE FRAGILE BACHELOR

by Gerald Nachman

Illustrations by John Boring

1⊖ TEN SPEED PRESS
Berkeley, California

These articles first appeared in the *San Francisco Chronicle*.

TEN SPEED PRESS
P.O. Box 7123
Berkeley, California 94707

Library of Congress Cataloging-in-Publication Data:

Nachman, Gerald.
　　The fragile bachelor / by Gerald Nachman; illustrations by John Boring
　　222 p.　cm.
　　"These articles first appeared in the *San Francisco Chronicle*"—T.p. verso.
　　ISBN 0-89815-289-5
　　1. Single men—United States.　2. Bachelors.　I. Title.
HQ800.4 U6N23　1989　305.3'890652—dc19
　　89-4420 CIP

Cover design by Fifth Street Design
Book design by Sarah Levin
Illustrations by John Boring
Typeset by Wilsted & Taylor

Printed in the United States of America

1　　2　　3　　4　　—　　92　　91　　90　　89

For the elusive Miss Right
(and all the runners-up)

TABLE OF CONTENTS

"In solitude be to thyself a throng."

—TIBULLUS

THANK YOU NOTES

It would be nice to say that this difficult, important and imposing book could not have been accomplished without the help of scores of people—diligent researchers, selfless librarians, generous and patient family members—but the sorry fact of it is, I did all the work myself. Nonetheless, I want to bestow bouquets of gratitude upon Bill German, executive editor of the *San Francisco Chronicle*, where these pieces first ran as "The Single Life," for encouraging the idea, promoting it and not interfering with it; to the *Chronicle* itself, for graciously allowing the pieces to be reprinted; to editor Lee Salem at Universal Press Syndicate, for giving the column national exposure and also for granting permission to reprint certain pieces; to features editor Rosalie Wright, for gently guiding the column around various pitfalls and potholes; to John Boring, who did the clever, often brilliant, silhouette drawings that accompanied the column and pulled unsuspecting readers into the first sentence whether they liked it or not; to Patti Breitman, editor-agent-cutup-tomato farmer-party giver-baseball fan-demon Scrabble player, whose good will, pretty good jokes, patter, patience and boundless enthusiasm begat the book and nursed it into print; and, to be sure, to various female friends, from Anna to Zelda, and male comrades in arms, for providing me with the irresistible raw material that kept the column humming right along. Let's all do it again real soon.

—*G.N.*

OPENING LINES

There is something undeniably shameless, vain and probably even stupid about describing the intimate details of one's private life in public, but, well, it's a living. Or was, anyway, for a year. Everyone wondered how and why I ever got started as a professional single person, and a lot of people wondered when all the agony would end.

Before I began writing about the sovereign, and messy, state of singlehood, nobody had ever done it before on a regular basis; I soon discovered why. Little did I suspect it was such a touchy subject and that, when I embarked on the column bursting with optimism, I was setting foot in a kind of fern-covered mine field.

Singledom, it turned out, combines the three great American unmentionables—sex, God and politics. The sex part is clear enough, but God and politics need some explaining: being unmarried is, to many people, sinful and subversive. Some are more or less contentedly single but just as many hate every minute of it and do not enjoy being reminded of it by some smartaleck columnist. Eventually, to keep my sanity, I devised a theory, as follows: The degree to which readers liked or despised the column depended on how much they enjoyed being single.

Those who were not crazy about the column would couch their thinly-veiled dismay in questions like, "So how much longer do you have to write about singles?," "Why are they making you do this?" or "Whose idea *was* it to write the column?"

Friends took pity on me and considered the column some sort of journalistic punishment, like writing obits. The general tone of their reaction was, "When are they going to let you out?"

The opposite attitude was expressed by colleagues who felt I was getting away with editorial murder, and who thought it extremely shrewd of me to have conned the paper into underwriting my social life—the ultimate expense-account scam. I had to endure endless winks, nudges and nasty wisecracks, like the editor who sidled over to me a week after I began the column and said, "Well, I hope you're at least getting laid a lot." Gentlemen eyed me enviously; ladies could only roll their eyes.

I am very much afraid the whole idea was mine. It occurred, like all great ideas of western man, from out of nowhere. There I was, sitting naively in the editor's office being asked what kind of a column I could come up with that wouldn't duplicate any other in the paper and also would be "very contemporary and San Francisco." In my boyish innocence, I blurted, "How about something to do with singles?" (at the time a newly discovered phenomenon). In what is a rare response among editors I've known, he perked up and, if I recall, smiled. And that, boys and girls, is how "The Single Life," as it was later called, got its weird little self born.

Nothing I've written in 30 years of columnizing has produced such strong positive and negative reaction from readers—not counting a wicked anti-rock piece and my heartless drubbing of *E.T.*

People either loved or hated the column, which was fine with me; at least everyone felt something about it. I had a wonderful time, with a couple of reservations. What I most disliked about the job was (1) being considered a singles guru, an expert who allegedly knew where all the perfect men and women were being kept, and (2) being regarded as some kind of male bimbo who spent my nights draped over a stool in singles bars.

The fact is, I avoided such doleful joints like the plague, dropping in only out of a sense of duty and leaving as soon as possible, my half-finished ginger ale still cold to the touch. In my year as an official single guy, I never spent more than 45 minutes in any singles bar at one time. It wasn't just the creeping-flesh factor that got me; it was the boredom. There's much less going on at singles bars than outsiders think—and thus, from a practical point of view, much less copy.

In many ways, it was the easiest kind of column I've ever written. Within an hour after I had the go-ahead to develop the concept, I had typed out 67 ideas. They must all have been sitting there, waiting to be summoned, crouching for 20 years in corners of my mind. Ideas appeared quickly, I suppose, because they came out of my own life as a practicing single person, from all those experiences of living alone and hacking away at solitude.

Every date, every phone call, every dish of Lean Cuisine, every anxiety and *faux pas* and little romantic triumph—each one was a column waiting to be written. Without realizing it, I'd been busily researching the job for decades, the ten years prior to my marriage and the eight years afterwards. So ideas were the easy part.

The hard part was trying to be fairly objective, honest and perhaps amusing about my personal single saga and not insult or maim anyone I knew in the process. People would say, in great awe, "You're awfully brave to expose your private life in public." Yes and no. You may be sure I heavily edited my real private life and only wrote about the things that wouldn't embarrass anyone I knew, or me.

By disguising incidents and personalities, I succeeded fairly well in not humiliating any date—not in print, anyway. I'm less sure about the other part, and undoubtedly came off as a jerk or a fool on a regular basis, about par for the course as a columnist; the willingness to parade your ego and look like an idiot in public is part of the job description. Probably I should have been more embarrassed about the whole thing, but I was having too much fun to think about it a lot, plus two deadlines a week.

Only once did I trip over the bounds of good sportsmanship and unwittingly cause someone to squirm. It was a woman I had met for a drink through the good offices of a dating agency and later wrote about (heavily altered) who recognized herself and called to complain, justifiably. No matter how carefully you fictionalize someone, if only she still recognizes who it is, it's one too many. After this little incident, I made sure that women I took out were aware what I did for a living; I often felt like an undercover agent. In every case, they were flattered to be a potential column, and in many cases women were upset if I *didn't* write about them. Usually, they would say with a coquettish giggle, "I better be careful or I'll wind up in your column!"

From the first column, I was besieged with ideas from fellow singles (my best source was dates ratting on past dates), and wherever I went people were only too eager to bend my ear with horror stories from their own single lives. Except on dates, I traveled under a thick cloak of anonymity and learned to eavesdrop like Bob Woodward. I perfected the investigative reporter's skill of ducking into men's rooms and behind potted plants to jot down funny lines and impressions. I must have filled 5000 restaurant receipt stubs and cocktail napkins with illegible quotes; when anyone gave me a business card, I'd palm it and use it as a notebook.

Readers not only gave me ideas about what to write but, if they learned who I was, told me *how* to write it. There were those (women usually) who felt I was a little too "flip" about the urgent state of singlehood, which to many unmarried people is a deadly serious business. Their feeling was, it's tough enough being single without having anyone make light of it. These, as I say, tended to be people who were miserable about their present condition and thought it unseemly of one of their own to discuss it in anything like a frivolous manner. To them, it was like joking about cripples.

I didn't intend to be mean but it struck me right away that the only approach to writing about single people was with a somewhat jaundiced, albeit sympathetic, eye; in fact, that's what appealed to me about the idea in the first place. Single people, some of them, tend to take themselves pretty seriously, at least in the area of relationships—the heart of singledom if not the whole of it.

As much as possible, I tried to veer away from romance and focus on the day-to-day nuts and bolts of living alone: dining solo, finding a home to nestle in during the holidays, eating in, entertaining yourself on Sundays, shopping for beds and dishes and lover's birthday gifts and appropriate St. Valentine's Day cards, going to a movie by yourself, always hoping to cover a range of experiences beyond the hugs and kisses. I may have succeeded too well, for after I'd been doing the column for half a year, someone complained, "There's not enough sex in your column." I took instant steps to remedy the situation only to have someone else ask me, a few months later, if I was also writing the Joe Bob Briggs column.

When I began, I assumed the pieces would bore anyone who was married but quickly discovered a secret cult of nonsingles who read the column, covertly, maybe to see how the disadvantaged lived (and make themselves feel better), or perhaps as an exercise in nostalgia, or even, in some cases, as sheer fantasy. One of my guiding precepts might explain it: we all come into the world single. (Another of my wise sayings: *Some are single by nature; others have singleness thrust upon them.*)

Anyway, something about singlehood lent itself to humor, much of it self-inflicted. My own haphazard dating life was funny enough without great elaboration, but the very notion of spending five or six hours with an almost total stranger of the opposite sex is already comical—not to mention the even zanier prospect of doing so regularly, on purpose, and trying to find a life mate in the process. Let me invoke Lincoln, if I may. When people asked him why he told so many jokes during the Civil War, he said, "I laugh that I should not weep."

One of the main surprises when I began the column was discovering there were almost no books on the subject of singleness, especially considering what a sprawling subculture (indeed, small independent nation) it's become. The books I dug up fell, with a thud, into two categories: deadly studies of unmarried people, with charts and graphs about buying power and socio-economic levels, and equally unreadable, depressingly cheerful books in the Where-the-Boys-(or -Girls)-Are genre.

Writing about singles turned out to be an inexhaustible topic, and I was always reminded by readers of the major areas I neglected—gays, widows, single parents, romance in the golden years, etc. My only excuse was that I was straight, unwidowed, childless and still had to pay full fare on the bus.

The built-in trap, which crosses all single lines and could also explain some of the resistance by certain readers, is that nobody likes being characterized—and stereotyped—as a "single," with all of its demoralizing, not to say sleazy, overtones—"swinging singles," "the singles scene," singles bars, Club Med, etc.

Singles have an image problem (there's even a piece about it in here somewhere), so I attempted to take on all the prominent singles cliches. In some paradoxical and maddening way, merely discussing them, or even mocking them, kept them alive. I'd beat my brains out telling what a sham some singles club was, or explain that a famous so-called singles supermarket was a great place to pick up groceries, only to run into some little lady at a party who would buttonhole me at the clam dip and growl, "I wish you'd stop writing about singles bars!" (I once tallied all the singles-bar pieces I'd done, and it came to about four out of 116 columns; if anything,

I'd underreported them.) I finally decided that people who thought I wrote about singles bars were not steady readers and thus, of course, were beneath contempt.

In time, however, I felt myself retracing my steps and repeating familiar themes, and decided, with a combination of reluctance and relief, to escape while I could, with my tattered image still intact, and tiptoed quietly into writing about things non-single. I miss it now and then, so when the urge is upon me I like to journey back into that strange, funny, *angst*-ridden land. My visa is still good, for Miss Right has not yet made her appearance. She's just being coy.

Now when I return to Singleville, as a tourist, I like to revisit some of my old chums who appear in these pages: Dr. Meyer Singleberg, the not-quite-renown relationship doctor; Guy Solo, the world's oldest bachelor; Phil Lander, God's gift to women (batteries not included); Marvin Waffler, the semi-committed man; Howie X, the never-say-die loser; and my two favorite long-suffering women pals, Vera Similitude and Nora Evergreen of the increasingly lowered expectations and perpetually rising hopes.

Being single, I eventually realized, is about surviving in a two-by-two world and doing it with as much grace, grit and wit as you can manage. Most do it surprisingly well, some stumble and flail about, and the rest of us are somewhere in between, depending on which day you happen to bump into us at the frozen food case.

In my columnist's mind's eye, I would envision single folks as a sturdy, plucky band of little Robinson Crusoes valiantly making a life of their own, living on nuts and berries around camp fires on a vast island surrounded by millions of curious native inhabitants who run around in pairs.

My job, as I saw it, was to show them they weren't really alone and maybe make them feel a little better about existing on that island until help arrives. Although the column ran on Tuesdays and Thursdays, I liked to think of myself as Friday, and the pieces in this book are a few of the footprints I left behind.

—Gerald Nachman
October 28, 1988

THE FRAGILE BACHELOR

SINGLISH SPOKEN HERE

Seeing: More serious than "dating" and less serious than "going with," as in: "I've been *seeing* Betty lately." Used as an infinitive, it indicates a new relationship, as in: "I'm starting *to see* Veronica."

Sort of Seeing Someone: Heavily involved with but starting to have doubts about, as in: "I'd love to go out but I'm *sort of seeing someone* right now."

Going With: Implies steadiness and exclusivity, as opposed to merely "dating," as in: "Jim's *going with* Jean but he's seeing Jane and also dating Joan."

Taking Out: A notch less serious than (but almost synonymous with) dating as in: "Hal's *taking out* Sue but he's also dating other people."

Involved: The penultimate state of togetherness, often lasting up to six months, as in: "Helen is very *involved* right now."

Serious About: More serious than *going with* but less serious than *involved*, as in: "Nathan is *serious about* Adelaide, but he's not ready to get involved."

Friend: A neuter person of the opposite sex who lacks a sexual identity, as in: "When I was in Boston, I saw a *friend*." Or, "I'm busy Saturday. I have this *friend* coming up from L.A." "Friend" repeated several times, preceded by "old," indicates a former lover.

Someone: Same as "friend"—an impersonal pronoun without gender, referred to in the Past Indefinite, as in: "I know *someone* who had that experience." Or, "I had lunch with *someone* in my office who . . ."

People: Plural of *friend* and *someone*, indicating one couple plus a male or female date, as in: "I have some *people* coming to dinner Tuesday."

Out-of-town Guests, Visitors (plural form only): Having an affair with a person from Cleveland, as in: "Gee, I have *guests* coming in Friday."

Appointment: More formal and suspect than "date," as in: "I have an *appointment* at 7."

My Accountant: Polite form of "honey," as in: "I have an appointment with my *accountant* tonight."

Busy Week: Indicates early throes of affair, as in: "This is a really *busy week* for me." Or, "It looks like I'm going to be *busy* all next week." Same as "jammed up," "tied up," "very hectic."

You *Seem* Very Healthy: Do you have herpes?

My Marriage Had Certain Problems: No sex for nine years.

Arrangement: Speaker is cheating on his/her mate, as in: "Rick and I have this *arrangement*."

I Have to Be Out of Town: If said rapidly, with the accent on "have," with no actual town mentioned, indicates speaker is having a wild weekend, as in: "Darn, Thursday *I have to be out of town*."

Big Day Tomorrow: No sex tonight, as in: "I have a *big day tomorrow*." This idiom takes various forms, such as: "It's a school night," "Don't tell me it's 10:15 *already*" and "Pumpkin time!"

Do You Live Alone?: Your place or mine?

I'd Love to See Your Apartment: Your place.

I Do Have a Boyfriend (Girlfriend): I don't sit home Saturday nights but I'm willing to be swept off my feet should you care to give it a whirl.

I See Someone on a Regular Basis: Same as above. (Note subtle usage of "see" and "someone.")

You Must Date A Lot: Do you have herpes?

Do You Like to Travel?: To Guadalajara, for instance? With me, for instance?

Special: Term of endearment, once used sparingly but now meaningless, as in: "You're a very *special* woman, Gwen—I mean Cicely."

Sex Is No Big Deal: Impotent, frigid, eunuch.

I'm Busy Weekends: My lover's in law school.

I'm Free Weekends: I'm having an affair with a married man (woman).

Home After Lunch: A nooner, as in: "Miss Moneypenny, I'll be *home after lunch* if anyone calls."

You *Seem* Like a Nice Guy: Are you gay, married, into drugs or four-legged creatures?

Fond Of or Care About: A way of avoiding the word "love," either out of coyness or cowardice, as in: "You know how *fond of* you I am, Tristan." "I *care about* you, too, Isolde."

RELATIONSHIPS PASSING IN THE NIGHT

Y OU'RE OUT on a date with this month's Ms. Semi-Right. You are in a restaurant and feeling pretty spunky. Fine food, vintage wine, superb lighting. You both look simply marvelous. The chatter seems to be progressing nicely. You're into second-stage chat—past the resumes and former marriages and into the basic hopes-and-dreams stuff.

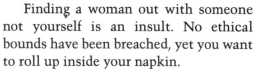

Everything's clicking right along until, suddenly, a familiar shadow crosses the room. Your eyes lock, your throat tightens. It is Ms. Semi-Right II, who is also out on a date (what nerve!) and will soon pass your table.

Finding a woman out with someone not yourself is an insult. No ethical bounds have been breached, yet you want to roll up inside your napkin.

Running into other people you're "seeing" can put a slight crimp in things and reveal singlehood as but a meaningless charade, a creaky merry-go-round. Do you nod? Wink? Blow a kiss? Run like crazy?

There is no reason to get rattled. You are all adults, right? No need for sweaty palms or trembling forks. With a deft head feint, it's possible to avoid her completely, but you have a date Friday. Pushing your spoon onto the floor and pretending to search for it lacks a certain heroic stature.

The correct thing, of course, is to face the music, leap up and, like a proper gent, introduce everyone. That's what Miss Manners would do. Manners are one thing; reality is another. One must be ready with at least a full minute's worth of solid supplemental talk.

You can't say, "Been here before?," since you've already been here together, adding to the shame of it all. You might comment on the parking or compare your lamb to her duck.

Another possibility is to wait until the woman is back at her table and then mumble that you see an "old friend" you ought to say hello to, vaguely implying that it's the gentleman you recognize.

The coward's way out—which I heartily endorse—is to simply nod politely and flash a roguish conspiratorial grin that says, "Aren't we two devils, though!" No words need be exchanged; neither date need wonder what's up, and you each have time to prepare a lavish explanation before laughing about it together Friday night.

One final possibility is to pretend to choke on a piece of meat, which will render you speechless and allow you to beat a hasty exit on a stretcher. This is known as the Nachman Maneuver and it has saved many a love life.

For stark terror, nothing beats running into one's ex-spouse. This has happened to me twice—the same ex, different dates. All ex-wives and husbands should remain in hiding forever as part of the final agreement.

Once, I was in New York at Sardi's and guess who popped out from behind a waiter but a long-lost niece who cried, "Uncle Jerry!" The purpose, of course, was to rattle Uncle Jerry.

Just as I was reeling from a niece I hadn't seen in ten years, who should loom up but Auntie herself, the First Mrs. N. A weird time was had by all, complete with frozen smiles, hollow jokes and stammered introductions. It was like a scene out of "I Love Lucy." All around me, I imagined people chuckling behind their menus.

The First Mrs. N. is famous for surprises. Not long ago she pulled another. At an art deco ball, a woman I couldn't quite see waved to me from across a crowded room—the lobby, actually, of a theatre. Probably some press agent I can't recall, I thought, waving vaguely. Yet why was this woman laughing?

The laughing woman turned out to be the First Mrs. N. We all shook hands, made small talk and I introduced the woman with me, who behaved impeccably. We all did. People always are real nice in emergencies.

Everyone acted chummy as we furiously sized each other up, checking for wrinkles, sags and signs of incipient decomposure. This seemed less an old sit-com than a scene from *Private Lives*, all of us straining to remain terribly cool and amusing and not utter anything that had even a tinge of innuendo, bad taste or jealousy. The First Mrs. N. did make one catty crack, but the score was tied when my date prodded a man to ask her to dance.

Everybody searched for a topic without overtones or undercurrents. I believe we ended up discussing the band a lot, but don't ask me. I wasn't quite there.

GUY'S GUIDE TO DINING IN

THERE ARE FEW more depressing sights than a single person's refrigerator. Actually, it's less of a refrigerator than a spare closet for old food.

Singles don't eat food, we accumulate it. We eat in spurts, never knowing when we'll be eating, or what, or often why.

We shop in bursts of optimism but forget to buy staples. We aren't quite sure what staples are. We exist on moldy bagels, forgotten cookies, tinny grapefruit juice, dead fruit, wilted Cheerios and, mostly, cheese.

Cheese is the single person's staff of life. Bread gets old too fast—often in as little as two weeks. I now have on hand about a month's worth of rye heels, which I can't bring myself to toss out.

In the event of a nuclear war, those heels could come in mighty handy. I've been known to make up extra meals, just to get rid of excess food before it rots.

Cheese is made to order for singles. If it gets stale, you can't quite tell—it just becomes, well, tangier. Also, cheese tastes like regular food—it's chewy and melts in the mouth. Lastly, it's easy to fix and may be eaten standing up, a common dining position among singles more accustomed to bars and dances.

The average single person's refrigerator contains jars of half-finished substances, many so old that they only can be positively identified by a crack crime lab.

My Kelvinator is full of staples like U-No bars, zipless root beer, eggs I'd rather not open and 17 jars of jam, each with one teaspoon of jam left—everything, that is, but actual living food.

This is because single people don't eat *meals*, per se. We eat snacks and leftovers, putting together inspired concoctions that only single people dare reveal to each other, dishes that cause mothers to shudder.

Yet most of the most inventive cooking being done today is by single people. We can create a lively meal out of anything that's around the house and hasn't yet turned to dust. Talk about survival techniques. Talk about *nouvelle cuisine*.

Even if it isn't, I pretend to manufacture a real meal by creating mock courses, lending an air of dinnerlike verisimilitude. When you're single, dinner at home doesn't actually count as dinner. It's almost a diet.

One night, I began with an appetizer of honey-roasted cashews, followed by a salad of Bob Ostrow fruit mold in a plastic carton. The entrée consisted of four-day-old tuna on nachos, with a side of chive cottage cheese, topped off with the last few scoops of praline ice cream; one nice thing about ice cream, it doesn't go stale on you after a few months. (What's a few inches of ice crystals?)

Notice that the above is an exotic mixture of both junk and gourmet food—a single person's balanced diet. Something old and something new, something borrowed and something blue (jack cheese, rye bread, tomato bisque soup).

A single person, you see, does all of his *serious* eating out. So if we're home, it's really an off night. We're between meals, as it were. If the sink is full, we may even skip dinner completely because we're all out of dishes.

DATING IN THE DARK

I T IS AGAINST human nature to blind date, but if you're single long enough you will finally succumb to it, always against your better judgment, kicking and screaming all the way to the doorbell.

Despite a universally lousy press and a checkered history, the blind date survives. I find this inspiring, a kind of affirmation of

man's eternal optimism and his faith in the dating gods—and women.

In many cases, the blind date is a last resort, a desperate move, often made in a weak moment, during a lean dating period when the only alternatives are a singles bar or a desert island. I don't know anyone who actively seeks out blind dates. That way lies madness.

Blind dating begins as charity work among contented couples who happen to Know Somebody Just Fabulous You Must Meet. My gut, admittedly gutless, reaction to this is: If they're so fabulous, why ain't they taken? Frequently, one is swept along by the enthusiasm of the moment, aided by the fixer-upper's wild promises and ecstatic endorsements.

Notwithstanding its low success ratio, the blind date retains a certain thrill, an anything-can-happen aura; there is that thousand-to-one shot that this may be the big It. One hears actual tales of people who met on blind dates and went on to lead happy, constructive lives together, improbable though it seems.

Ideally, blind dates should be world-class great sports and possess gentle, forgiving natures. They must also be terrific actors, should the worst occur. They ought not to carry sharp instruments on their person.

The first rule of blind dating is to pin the fixer-upper to the floor when he or she begins describing said fabulous person. Do not accept blurry character descriptions and sketchy verbal portraits. When someone says, "She's a fun person," demand examples: When was she fun and why?; define "fun."

Fuzzy phrases like "a nice smile," "a great woman" or "a terrific talker" may be code words meaning "goofy," "homely" or "boring." Insist on specifics. Grill the go-between. Watch for weasel classified ad words like "sweet," "attractive," "bright" and "high energy," which takes in four-fifths of the single population. Beware, too, of all modifiers, such as "rather pretty" and "deceptively smart" and "large-boned."

When women begin describing hair in detail, watch out. "She's got great red hair!" somebody once raved, neatly omitting all other non-great features. Someone else was described as "a real character, but you'll like her." That "but" spoke volumes.

Never take the word of a best friend, most of all a female friend. Women invariably err on the side of beauty. A woman's concept of "adorable" includes everyone from Jessica Lange to Roseanne Barr.

Women often mean inner beauty. A man has nothing *against* inner beauty, but not until a modicum of outer beauty has been firmly established. If another man is present, get a second opinion.

Once a woman told me about someone I should meet. "She's gorgeous!" crowed her friend. "Really?" I asked the husband, who said, "Hmmm, I wouldn't say 'gorgeous.' *Attractive*." Attractive is not in the gorgeous ballpark.

Once you've agreed to a blind date, there is a need to make the crucial phone call, a mine field of exotic dreams. A basic rule of blind dating is to keep the call brief; a two-hour talk drains away any mystery.

There is a tendency to say everything on the phone that should be saved for the date, which will need all the help it can get and rarely lives up to the phone call. A sexy voice can induce sublime fantasies. This is called the Conrad Effect. When William Conrad played Matt Dillion on radio, he sounded like James Arness looked.

One man I know was tempted to propose marriage to a blind date on the phone. He went through the formality of a date, one of the worst in dating history. Once the voices came face to face, it was all over. Both parties had worked much too hard to sound cute and funny and tantalizing on the telephone, doing all sorts of irreversible damage. The date itself was a calamity, especially since they had expected to fall in love no later than dessert.

He felt like suing her for misrepresentation. "She *sounded* so adorable," he groaned. "Her voice seemed thinner and much blonder."

THOSE AWFUL ROOMERS

S OMETHING THERE IS that doesn't love a roommate—me, for one. I don't mean a spouse or a lover. I mean a joint-householder of the same or other sex, a person who shares board but not bed.

I haven't had a roommate since college, unless you count one wife and one involvee. Given the choice of a rat hole or a roommate, a roomie is preferable, if not by a whole lot.

A roommate has all the problems of a spouse and few of the joys. No matter who the roommate, or whatever its gender, it eventually comes down to turf battles, whether it's for wall space, refrigerator shelves or psychic terrain. Then, too, there's the matter of personal habits—not yours, which are just fine; other people's, which are, of course, hideous.

Having a roommate, even someone you might love outdoors, sounds like the most perverse living arrangement possible. I am amazed so many people can make it work, or even tolerate it without turning on each other within days. Love and sex are difficult enough, but try coping with someone else's mangy towels and see how long you last.

Recently, two women at my office were squabbling over posters that one person had hung on the wall and that the other person loathed, claiming that the wall was also hers. She called into question not only aesthetic taste but geographical boundaries.

With roommates, this is the very stuff that must be hammered out on a daily basis, if I recall my old rooming-house days. And I do—with a shiver. Mostly what I remember is how the tiniest infraction of the rules, spoken or unspoken, could lead to major battles. When you live with someone, all-out war is only a dish-rag away. You live in a constant state of détente.

If there's no actual friction, it's easy enough to create some to keep things lively. In college I lived with three guys, two of whom slept late, class or no class. I would tiptoe about, getting dressed as quietly as possible and, thought I, being a veritable mouse.

Not to John. "Could you walk a little quieter?" John finally asked, the impertinent twit. "I *am* walking quietly," I claimed. What to me was padding-about was, by his standards, a herd of rhino. "Can't you wear socks until you leave?" he asked, burying his face in a pillow.

Another roomie objected to my sliding coins off the dresser into my palm, a fairly harmless habit. It was just something I did, like wearing shoes in the house. Suddenly, it was no mere habit; it was a shot heard 'round the room.

To a roommate, even your most innocent act can be (and often is) construed as a personal affront, if not a way to get his goat. There is a good deal of goat-getting when one person tries to live as two.

Then, of course, there is the ugly matter of disappearing food, leading to scenes out of *The Caine Mutiny*—i.e. whether someone is eating more than his share of the food bill.

To get even, you find yourself eating extra meals, gobbling up your rightful 50 percent of the strawberry cheesecake, so you're not left with only a third—even if you don't much feel like strawberry cheesecake that night.

One of my old college foursome would fix himself a fried egg sandwich late at night, leading to a philosophical debate on whether a midnight snack constitutes a bona fide meal. This was a crucial, indeed legal, point, because if it was *not* a legitimate meal, it meant that the person washing dishes that week was under no moral obligation to soak the fried egg plate, pan and fork. As I recall, this one went all the way to the Circuit Court of Appeals.

If the space squeeze doesn't get you, the time constraints will—time in the shower, time on the phone, time in the kitchen, time with the TV, the stereo. "How long will you be in there?" can take on a nasty edge if not said in the proper tone of voice (a shade too much emphasis on "long" is all it takes).

In the matter of decor, you may as well resign yourself to the fact that everybody else has lousy taste. Eventually, I simply gave up on the canvases my roommates chose to display (Miss April, Miss October, Picasso's Don Quixote, a Paris travel poster, a Pac-10 football schedule).

In rebellion, I opened my own gallery off in a corner of an adjoining roomlet, where I finally set up a make-shift bedroom, hung my tasteful Corots and scooped as many coins off the dresser as I damn pleased. It wasn't much but it was home.

UGLY SINGLE MYTHS

E VEN IN THESE enlightened times, something unwholesome still clings to the single person. Or un-person.

The very word "single" has a slightly shameful ring. People cringe from being designated "single," as yuppies cower from that dreaded label. It denies us our last vestige of individuality to be plunked down in a group of nomadic nametags.

Filling out an IRS form, I shy from the "single" box. I prefer "divorced," which suddenly sounds more stable than single; anything would, even "married lunatic." "Single" somehow suggests a rootless, even soulless, person—a guy without a country. "Unmarried" has a shade more dignity but indicates, if not a flawed nature, someone looking out the window in a lonely flat. "Unmarried" sounds monkish or spinstery.

Even worse than "single" is its swinging big brother, "Singles," which has a touch of the zany and decadent about it. Someone who readily admits to being single cringes at the word "singles."

Still, a certain mystique clings to the term. Married people assume we're out each night, partying until dawn, drinking and prowling the streets. I, of course, try to encourage this notion. If a married man in the office sees me shaving at 5 o'clock, he winks, "Another hot date, eh?" I merely grin enigmatically, never disclosing that I'm going to Mom's. Why ruin his good time?

Singles fall somewhere between first- and second-class citizens, yet our numbers are growing. We have become a nation of singles with political clout. We're an Economic Force, an actual "market," just like teenagers. We gained a tad more respect when the ACLU published a booklet, "The Rights of Single People." (Cohabitation is illegal in 13 states, etc.)

Yet singles still carry a stigma. We're indulged and suspect. We're regarded, no matter what anyone says, as a crime against nature, an assault on the species, an affront to the sanctity of marriage, a monkey wrench in the scheme of life, a societal glitch.

People think we're unserious. The single man is a parody of boyhood. Single women threaten motherhood. We won't grow up, they sneer. We are viewed as aging collegiates, labeled Peter Pans and Wendys, Cinderellas and Princes, selfish beasts who aren't pulling our load, a threat to the nuclear family. We're the enemy within.

Singles belong to a privileged underclass, Yuppies Without Partners. We're not a recognized institution, like wedlock. There's no such state as "holy singlelock." Single parenthood is courageous, bachelorhood a lark.

Singledom is a rung below living together. Living alone had a few chic weeks in the mid-'70s, when solitude and celibacy tried for a comeback, but now we're back at our traditional forlorn stand.

Single fathers and unwed mothers have a certain brave dignity, and even the bachelor woman has finally won her medals—no longer the frumpy old maid, she's now the smartly dressed career woman on the move.

Bachelors, both confirmed and un-, are the lowest rung on the singles ladder. Single women get to claim Gloria Steinem, Jeane Kirkpatrick and Oprah Winfrey as role models. Single men have no role models, just models—George Hamilton, Warren Beatty, Don Johnson, never Ralph Nader, Ed Koch or Gandhi.

All of which feeds singles guilt. Many single people feel, deep down, that they should be *unsingle*—married, living with someone, bigamous, asexual, dead, anything but (ugh) single. Singles may be more than waiting for marriage, but it's still less than doubles.

Couples don't understand. They think it's all whoopee out here, while they're at home in their snug suburban cottages, having kids and dinners and filing jointly.

Why does it seem that whenever a gunman or assassin makes the news, he sounds suspiciously like me—a man living alone who "keeps to himself and nods hello to the neighbors." Look at John Wilkes Booth, John Hinckley Jr., Richard Speck, James Earl Ray, Billy the Kid, Sirhan Sirhan, John Dillinger, Jesse James, Ted Bundy—friendly neighbors all, but single guys each and every one.

RAISED HOPES, LOWERED EXPECTATIONS

N ORA EVERGREEN, the everywoman I know who's nearing 40, mentioned the other night that she's decided to lower her eligible-male standards.

"And you're starting with me, is that it?" I said, smiling thinly.

"No, but I'm seriously considering a major policy change," Nora said. "I can't hold out forever for Mr. Right. I was just 38. I'm willing to negotiate. I'll settle for Mr. Not So Bad."

For starters, she's decided to reduce her height requirement.
"The Landmarks Commission will be glad to hear that," I said.

At one time, Nora, who is 5-foot-9 without heels, would go out
only with men six feet or higher.

"When I was 30, I wouldn't even consider a guy under 6-foot-
2. When I turned 35, I had an affair with a guy six feet tall; I decided
I'd been too fussy. Now, I'm down to 5-foot-11. Stop me at 5-9."

I asked her how else she'd lowered her expectations.

"Well, I don't care anymore if he smokes, and he doesn't have
to make at least $50,000 a year."

"What's your new asking price?"

"I'm holding out for forty thou, but between you and me, I'll go
as low as thirty-eight five—if he's perfect otherwise."

"So you still demand a dreamboat?"

"Well, yes and no," said Nora. "I'll take a good solid yacht, if
he's not too creaky. I'm also expanding my previous age limits. Before, I insisted the man be at least five years older than I but not
more than 15."

"And now?"

"I'm willing to look at anything between 35 and 60—but just
look, you understand."

"Well, it's good to see you've become less inflexible," I said.
"Maybe that was your problem before."

"Life is a series of compromises," Nora sighed. "I always knew
that before, of course, but I never thought it included men. Or me,
of all people."

"The important thing, I guess, is that he be a nice guy," I said.

She smiled. "My definition of 'nice' also has been slightly ex-
panded. Ten years ago, when I said 'nice,' I actually meant wonderful. Now I think 'nice' is quite acceptable—especially after the
last two 'wonderful' guys I went with turned out to be crumbs.
Nice isn't so bad. Assuming, of course, he has his own hair."

"Ah, so you're still holding out for certain details."

"Oh, definitely. I haven't sold out completely. I'm just much
more . . . *realistic*. But I'm still pretty adamant on a few points."

"Like what?"

"Well, pets and children."

"You don't allow any pets?"

"A small cat is OK, but no dogs, tropical fish or birds. And I'm a stickler for children. He really has to like kids."

"How many?"

"In the old days, I insisted on three, but now I could be talked down to one."

"Well, it sounds like you're definitely increasing your chances of meeting Mr. Not So Bad."

Nora frowned, "I know. That's what scares me most of all."

SINGLE-MINDED RESOLVES

MY FIRST RESOLUTION was not to write a New Year's resolution column, an admittedly cheap and easy device to get out of writing what we call a real piece—one with compound clauses, transitions, structure, punctuation and all sorts of wonderful things.

Until then, however, I firmly resolve in the current year to:

• Make no more firm resolves and face up to my basically spineless nature.

• Visit a health club (to improve spine) or a dance club, where the action is reputed to be.

• Devise a less awkward and painful way of holding hands in movies.

• Clean out the back of my refrigerator and find out who's living in there, rent-free.

• Stop impugning my refrigerator, which isn't as bad as I make out.

• Go to at least one singles bar, because that's what people expect of us wild and crazy single people, and stay a full hour.

• Learn the name of a roguish sounding drink that I can order. Learn to sip it without making a face.

• Make up my mind, once and for all, about opening car doors for women and strictly adhere to this policy.

• Have a regular table at a well-known, or even unknown, restaurant.

• Practice my answering machine voice so I sound warm and amusing and yet somehow convey my understated good looks and *savoir-faire.*

• Have the nerve to order a cheeseburger even after the waiter has gone through 27 daily specials.

• Order at least one daily special this year.

• Quit making nasty cracks about babies, who probably can't help it.

• Spice up my life story a little, if only to keep me awake over dinner, and put it all on a cassette to distribute to upcoming dates so they will have plenty of time to prepare pertinent questions and a few follow-ups.

• Stop saying to women in the Maybe Zone, "We really should have lunch and stop saying we will."

• Discover a terrific, quiet, little after-hours out-of-the-way place that nobody but me knows about.

• Break no more than two dates next year, and only for dire emergencies.

• Think up better dire emergencies.

• If forced to break a date, consider telling an actual truthhood: "I'm in a grumpy mood," "I'd rather watch *Moonlighting,*" "I totally forgot that Sunday is my regular night for contemplating the futility of life."

• Take a class at a cooking school and learn the proper methods of basting, boning and sautéing tuna melts.

• Stop falling hopelessly in love at stoplights with women in little green Datsuns.

• Get into more substantive issues on dates than the crucial differences between New York, Chicago and California pizza.

- Cease judging women on the basis of punctuality and/or their taste in comedians, remembering that even Meryl Streep probably runs a little late and that Eleanor Roosevelt might not have been amused by Albert Brooks.
- Stop using "fun" as an adjective and never again employ the following yupisms, even in jest: "Go for it," "Gimme a break," "You got it," "Check it out," "We're talking . . . ," "Lighten up."
- Learn to dance something faster than the fox trot, even if it's only the waltz.
- Wear my wild purple paisley tie in public at least once; also, see how I look in a bowtie.
- Update my little black book with ruthless abandon.
- Devise a clever way to get to Debra Winger.
- Try a Lean Cuisine dish other than glazed chicken with rice and vegetables; consider Le Menu.
- Stop rearranging the magazines on my coffee table so that the New Yorkers and Vanity Fairs cover up the Peoples.
- Marry somebody really neat.

A RAMBLIN' KINDA GUY

UNTIL YOU'VE SPENT a night in Rutland, Vt., you have not known true singleness, alone as alone can get. You stare solitude in the eye and wait to see who blinks first.

The prospect of a month on the road was ripe with Kerouac-esque possibilities, Hemingway high adventure, or, failing that, humble Thoreauvian contemplation. All your really major wanderers and wayfarers were lonely guys and turned a pretty nice buck at it.

It was in this back-to-nature mood that I set out from New York by Buick Skylark for ten days into the heart of New England, a single odyssey full of fantasy and the thrill of the unknown. I would study the leaves; I would go for tramps through the woods—parking lots, anyway.

I would, God forbid, get in touch with my feelings. I would think major thoughts. I would speak to nobody for days except to mumble, "The boiled beef, butter squash and Indian pudding, please."

For days, the only voices I heard, aside from my own inner babble, were innkeepers, turnpike toll takers and waitpersons; my banter went unnoticed, as did I. By the third day, I was striking up earnest conversations with gift-shop ladies. Roadside apple sellers seemed desperate for human contact. They didn't just want to peddle cider and Vermont cheddar; they craved my ear, and I theirs.

With only my thoughts for company, I ran out of conversation in Lenox, Mass. The mind began playing tricks. A blowsy teenage girl at a Friendly's ice cream parlor began to assume the qualities of Melanie Griffith.

An innkeeper's wife, lolling seductively in the next room watching "Wheel of Fortune," induced flashbacks of *The Postman Always Rings Twice*. Did a guide at The Breakers in Newport want to be taken away from all this, or did I?

My cool loner image crumbled in Northampton, Mass. I wanted talk—small, big, medium. I eagerly engaged fellow bed-and-breakfasters in fervent discussions of alternate routes and the ferry times from Woods Hole.

In Boston, I stumbled into Friday's, a singles bar, but was appalled at the scene, like a '60s movie. I'd forgotten such places existed and fled to Wirth's, an ancient beer hall, for sauerbraten; it was empty but honest.

The lone traveler is grateful for any tiny diversion. A black and white TV set is a gala occasion. The major social event my first week was a night watching *Death of a Salesman* holed up in Bennington, Vt., Willie Loman's old territory, where I, too, felt the silent terrors of traveling salesmen.

In Manchester, Vt., I seriously considered a bingo game. Outside Essex, Conn., I almost caved in and went to a movie, a cop-out. Would Thoreau go to a movie? Scenery is great, but there's precious little communing with nature after six, when the fall foliage closes for the day.

There are certain advantages to solo travel. One need never

comment aloud on the scenery. You may gasp or not. There's no pressure to visit a whaling museum if the Tennis Hall of Fame seems more fun. I snubbed major landmarks, giving Plymouth Rock ten minutes, which was stretching it. I drove through seedy Provincetown, where a hooker on a bike blew kisses at me.

Flying solo, I became an ace navigator, map reader and change maker (it's against New York state law to be without exact change for every human transaction). I did miss having someone to laugh at my jokes and to handle embarrassing questions: "Ask that man if we're in New Hampshire."

I lost all identity and became anybody. Did I still have fingerprints? A shadow? I felt like The Fugitive. Checking into inns, I tried not to look like a serial killer, only to grow suspicious of innkeepers. A geezer who warily rented me a cabin on Cape Cod (once he was convinced I had no pets hidden in the trunk) became a stubbly Norman Bates: "So it's just yerself then?" I envisioned morning headlines reading: *"B&B Slayer Strikes Again!"*

In Cambridge, Mass., too close to Salem for comfort, a spooky lady innkeeper told me there was no need for bedroom locks. She proved harmless, unlike my bed, a lethal stock-like device discarded by the puritans made of a thin mattress and a board. I limped away.

You can't be dependent on the kindness of strangers, even with traveler's checks. Singles must rely on basic survival skills for diversion. Dinner took all night: an hour to scan dog-eared menus provided by the inn ("Captains Courageous—Serving Greater Gloucester Since 1978!"); an hour to cruise the area, weighing various quaintness factors; two hours to eat; an hour to find a Tastee Freeze for a nightcap.

There are no single people in the woods. It's Couplesville, border to border. My evening's entertainment consisted mainly of listening to tired piano-bar players plinking out oldies but baddies and reading books in my bedroom that were more atmosphere than literature—*The Barns of Vermont*, a 1948 Book-of-the-Month club selection by James Cozzens, or the occasional modern best seller (*Jonathan Livingston Seagull, Passages*).

I became fluent in postcardese, not just to make contact with home but as amusement, scribbling jaunty messages to persuade everyone that I was having a heck of a swell time. After a week, I felt like Robinson Crusoe (what did he do about laundry?) and began counting the hours until I could return to New York City, where being single has some real status.

MAKE YOUR BED
AND LIE IN IT

TELEVISION ANCHOR Diane Sawyer once told an interviewer that for years her bed consisted of a mattress thrown on the floor of her "bedroom."

Not surprising. Sawyer, albeit rich and famous, was, like many singles, unwilling to buy an entire bed. Presumably this changed when she moved to "60 Minutes," got decent hours and could afford a box spring. She married not long thereafter.

This is the old Mattress-on-the-Floor Syndrome, a telltale sign of Singlethink, of the restless wandering unwed who are unwilling to commit to so much as a bed, let alone a mate. Married people own major beds. Many singles sleep on mattresses. This is because, in their heads, most single people are still in college. Or else they're stewardesses. Stewardesses are the nation's leading nonpurchasers of headboards. Presumably they can sleep anywhere, even standing up.

People who sleep on mattresses also make bookcases out of bricks and boards, hang Bruce Springsteen posters on their living room walls and use throw-pillows as chairs. The floor mattress is a dead home-furnishings giveaway, one you won't see in Architectural Digest.

Such people are not yet able to commit to a full-size bed. They're stymied by things like, how big a bed should it be? How fancy? What style? Should it have a footboard *and* a headboard? What about nightstands, armrests, quilts and other beddy-bye gear?

The first thing one must do is to get out there and purchase an actual bed to go with the mattress, with a footboard. The works. A bed makes you feel better right away and much less like you're in a Munich youth hostel.

If someone is still 43 years old and continues to sleep on a mattress in the corner of a bedroom, he or she has failed too face certain facts.

Fact: A bare mattress is depressing to visitors, especially Mom and Dad and potential spouses. It smacks of commune life, of beach houses and hippie pads, of dorms and the brig, of camping out. A mattress looks sloppy and unmade. There's no way to make a lone mattress seem neat and tidy. A cot is better, a hammock, even a sleeping bag.

Fact: A mattress is a daily reminder of one's singletudinous state, of life afloat on the floorboards of fate.

Fact: A mattress on the floor makes one aware, twice a day, that one is bedless and thus not yet a truly grown-up person. Nobody can take seriously someone who sleeps on a mattress.

The Mattress-on-Floor factor had much to do with Jerry Brown's inability to win higher office. A young swinging governor who dates rock stars may sleep on the floor. A senator may not. The mattress is what did Brown in and led to his split with Linda Ronstadt, just an old-fashioned girl who craved a brass bed.

Beds, need I remind you, are a major aspect of single life. Couples sleep in the same bed for fifty years but single people must learn to cope with a vast array of, well, sleeping arrangements.

Some people can only sleep in one bed, their own. I am such a person. I have tried to be a good sport about this, but strange beds are just that. Bedwise, I'm a regular Goldilocks. I find them either too small, too high, too lumpy, too silky or too hot. Often they come equipped with cats or dogs and a bedful of bears and bunnies.

You are what you sleep. A rumpled bed suggests an unmade personality. The four-poster reveals sturdy Yankee values. A gauzy canopy hints at a romantic nature. A waterbed indicates a former wild-and-crazy person still trying to get his or her act together.

The question of bed size is of vital importance in a relationship. Anything less than queen-size may mean trouble. Find someone with a king-size bed, a sure sign of a generous nature, someone who will give you your own space (and pillow).

A queen-size bed is the bare minimum if we're talking serious sleeping. Double beds are for recreational use. If you've got two flailers or one turner and one tosser, you've got major problems, a pair who will wake up tired and cross. If one person is a cuddler and the other feels cramped, the future is not real bright.

Troubles in bed—not even counting sex—include pillows (too many, not enough, too fat, too thin, too downy, too bumpy) and covers (too few, too fluffy, too heavy, too slippery, too fuzzy). Just for starters.

A major area to be hammered out is who gets which side. There are wall people and rug people, open window vs. closed. There also are night-light people and pitch-dark people, curtains-pulled people and mole people, cats-on-the-bed people and no-pets-allowed people.

The best bed, I am very much afraid, is your own. Be it ever so chilly, there's no bed like home.

SECOND DATE MALAISE

THERE IS A phenomenon that, until just last week, I did not know existed, a condition that Dr. Meyer Singleberg, my relationship doctor, calls Second Date Blahs.

Observes Dr. Singleberg: "It may happen on the first date, sometimes the third date, or the ninth date, but what happens is the same no matter when it occurs:

"One is aware of a vaguely doleful feeling, accompanied by ringing in the ears and perhaps a tingling sensation in the fingers, as a little cloud passes overhead and threatens to rain on your relationship."

He says the Second Date Blahs more often strike those who have had too many second dates—i.e., your older, mature, gnarled single. "It consists of a dimly felt sense that things need to shift into a new, more definite, even intimate mode or there's no point

DR. SINGLEBERG

JB

in going on with a pleasant but futureless charade, endless replays of Date I."

He adds, "The naive or newly single is content to put in more time—often hundreds of dates—whereas your veteran single usually can tell on Date I if there's going to be a Date II by the end of the house salad."

A second date has more riding on it, he notes. The first date, you're busily panning for those nuggets of personality and past lives; this is enough to make an evening. By Date II, though, a certain reality sets in, a need to progress from Polite Exchanges to Distinct Possibility, followed by Lingering Dread.

Dr. Singleberg points out, "You're afraid you may run out of material—jokes, questions, amusing biographical anecdotes—by the middle of the second date. Usually, there's much more at stake the second time around."

He claims second dates try harder. "It's time to reach a semitentative conclusion about the other person and whether said person is about to have a part in your life, with songs and dances, or just fade into that vast crowd scene of first dates."

All of this stuff is floating in the air, little dust motes of doubts, which tend to gather into a small cloud no bigger than a woman's hand just as you pull into a parking place.

First dates have a certain built-in tension, he explains, but it's more like curiosity, the Thrill of the Unknown. Second dates are more free form. You're both out there on a wink and a prayer.

"The longer you're single, the more first dates you have and the fewer second dates," says Dr. S. "I can't document this but I would guess that the number of second dates decreases in direct proportion to one's years."

He adds: "The more first dates, the better you get at picking up signs, hints of latent weirdness. You learn to isolate major problem areas. It no longer takes 57 dates to realize that someone is, in fact, a jerk, no matter how cute they appear at the Xerox machine."

After a while, says Dr. Singleberg, you pick up on creepiness rather more quickly, on the phone even, and reach quicker conclusions, like: *This person is indeed sexy but also a total disaster.*

He folded his hands and went on: "On the first evening, if you've been at it a while and paying attention, all this gets fed into what we call your Video Dating Terminal. If the printout is basically positive, you then move onto the next, crucial Second Date—which is more like the seventh date for those with 253 dates under their belt."

Dr. Singleberg took out a chart and said, "After the age of 40, each date counts as seven."

He says all this accounts for those nagging Second Date Blahs. "Or it may be something else: fear and trembling, a feeling that either (1) you like the person and sense that he/she is less taken with you; or (2) you realize you like each other but you are not up to a major involvement at this point in time."

Whereupon, you wonder, Why am I dating in the first place if I don't want to find a lovely and talented person? Am I one of those frauds I keep reading about? Where is this relationship going to end? Is there any purpose to my tawdry little life? When am I going to get serious and grow up? Why can't I make a few decisions for a change? Who do I think I am, anyway?

Dr. Singleberg frowned. "The second date forces you to look at all these things—and this is what brings on the malady known in the profession as Second Date Blahs."

Is there a cure? "No, but it can be controlled by careful evasion. My advice is to delay answering all such major questions until the 37th date, when there's a good chance you'll be married to the person and not have to confront such weighty issues ever again."

PSST! WANNA MEET A NICE FRIEND?

W HEN IT COMES to meeting tall dark strangers, one is often dependent on the kindness of friends.

This, anyway, is the accumulated wisdom of recent women I've talked to, one of whom claims, "All the interesting men I've met have been through friends." So forget dating agencies, forget personal ads, forget parties, forget bars, forget chance encounters at checkout stands and bumping cutely into people coming off elevators, like in the movies.

What this means is that people who need people have been going about it all wrong. They have been trying to increase their dating circle when they should have been widening their circle of friends. What we need are fewer parties and more pals.

This changes the entire focus. Why beat your brains out when you can have people beating their brains out for you? Let your friends be your dating agency; it's cheaper and has more dignity.

The thing about friends is, they are sure to look out for you and have a fairly wide old-boy-girl network. Remarks one woman, "I've met many more men through other women than on my own." No, not rejects or old lovers, but viable men with actual good jobs who were none of the big three: weird, married or gay.

Says one newlywed woman: "I'm in the odd position of checking out men—not for myself but for my unmarried friends. Now that I'm paired off, I'm expected to help others in their search for Mr. Right." Noblesse oblige and all that.

One trouble with friends is that they know you too well and may protect you from intriguing types by too fine a pre-screening. As one woman admits, "Right now, my men friends are too short, too young and riddled with phobias and quirks. They're fine as friends, but unsuitable for relationships with the women I know."

Yet possibly those very quirks and fears are what make some-one someone. Otherwise, would you fix up Hamlet? Van Gogh? Venus de Milo? And with the right woman, maybe a young short macho guy, like Napoleon, could grow.

One possible problem is that close friends may be protecting their friends from you. A go-between is like a double agent—you can't be sure who he's working for.

Your friends know all the bad stuff about you that someone won't discover for many months, maybe years, things a friend doesn't want to be held responsible for. It's like selling a colleague your car, knowing it has some peculiar noises and overheats on long trips.

Friends have seen your narrow, stupid, intolerant sides. They know you hate kids and Greek food and are a grouchy driver. Or they may take all this into account and realize that, deep down, you're not a bad sort as narrow, stupid guys go. Friends are friends because they're willing to ignore all the bad stuff and don't care how odd you look.

I've been fixed up—more often, set up ("There's someone com-ing to dinner I think you'll like")—but the results are mixed. Often the person you're touted on is sitting next to someone you would cross hot coals for, whom your so-called pal failed to mention. Later, confronted with this, said friend cries, "That monster?!"

I admit that while I'm terribly intrigued and flattered by the idea that somebody thinks anyone is right for me, I also have a built-in defense system, comparable in many ways to the MX, only much more awesome.

So when I meet the lucky person, I'm immediately hunting for flaws, weaknesses, problem areas and incompatibilities, instead of just letting her entire personality wash over me, as I would normally.

I am also wondering what my friend sees in me. Why did he think this other soul was a match for my own personality? Then I go over my probable selling points and sterling features, specu-lating on the sales pitch the other person got. I may even try to impersonate the character I hope has been outlined—charming, witty, incredibly attractive, wealthy beyond riches—a swell catch, in brief.

One problem with dating, rarely cited, is that there's no time to make new friends. Someone should open a video buddy agency for people who have plenty of dates but are in the market for more close friends.

I suppose this is one reason they invented marriage. Viewed objectively, it's not a bad deal: For the price of one individual, you get a friend and a date forever and need never worry where to go after the movie.

THE FAST-FOOD GOURMET

A S A GOURMAND with a palate just slightly less developed than the Cookie Monster, I am naturally addicted to all TV and radio cooking shows.

Frugal Gourmet Jeff Smith, Julia Child, the microwave guy and his band of strolling players and now my latest whim, the chic, mysterious French lady known only as "Madeleine"—all sustain

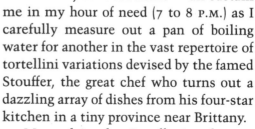

me in my hour of need (7 to 8 P.M.) as I carefully measure out a pan of boiling water for another in the vast repertoire of tortellini variations devised by the famed Stouffer, the great chef who turns out a dazzling array of dishes from his four-star kitchen in a tiny province near Brittany.

Many claim that Stouffer is a descendant of Escoffier, if not Clarence Birdseye himself.

True, I may only be fixing frozen pasta, tuna on toast or creamed spinach *au plastique* but, in my mind, I am whipping up a delicate souffle or an exotic steamed fish with fennel seeds, whatever they may be. I must remember to pick up some fennel seeds soon.

As I go about my mundane tasks, I am riveted by the video chefs' expertise and the nonchalance with which they knock out five-course meals while keeping up a line of amusing chatter.

Last week, for instance, as I gripped a can opener to open a tin of Bumblebee tuna, I imagined a camera zooming in on my hands to illustrate the dexterity with which I twist the key and, in six deft moves, have the lid open and—*voila!*—am neatly depositing succulent pink tuna fish flecks into a Pyrex bowl.

As I reach for the Miracle Whip, I say to my transfixed viewers: "You may use either a teaspoon or a fork to gently lift the creamy mayonnaise blend from the jar and quickly fold it into the tuna, taking care to stir evenly and to break up any remaining chunks of tuna."

With an assured but intimate chuckle, I add, "Those little rascals do tend to stick together!"

Meanwhile, as I allow the tuna to "breathe" on the counter, I take the cottage cheese out of the refrigerator and pop off the lid with my thumbnail, in a quick upward flipping motion, being sure that no curds drop into the tuna or on the floor, then add four Del Monte pear halves, which I arrange in an attractive manner around the edge of the mound of cottage cheese.

My voice-over narrator smacks his lips and says with awe: "Chef Gerald shows what artistic culinary feats are possible with a little imagination!"

Tonight, I inform my unseen audience, I will lightly toast two slices of Columbo sourdough bread on which I shall then spread the tuna—after gently buttering the toast with a spread that should be, but rarely is, at room temperature.

As I patiently explain to my viewers, always remember to remove your tub of Parkay a good 15 minutes before spreading, lest you tear holes in the toast, a little trick I picked up from none other than the legendary Chef Wonder.

Once the tuna has been applied, I remark to the folks at home that they may want to add a slice of Muenster cheese to bring out the flavor of the tuna. Once again, blast it, I appear to be out of fennel seeds.

Ah, it appears my pot of water is boiling! Time to dunk the frozen pouch of creamed spinach.

As I firmly explain, this must be done without splashing hot water on you, yet always making sure that the plastic pouch is totally submerged, turning the packet periodically for 14 minutes, so that the spinach cooks through evenly, taking care not to burn your fingers. Those of you out there who like your frozen spinach *al dente* may wish to remove it after 12 minutes. To each his own!

When your spinach is finished, lift it out and (making sure not to cut your thumb!) snip one corner and let the spinach gurgle out onto the plate, careful that it doesn't ooze over into the tuna sandwich. Two plates *may* be necessary.

As I advise my audience, it's a wise idea to first empty the creamed spinach and *then* lay the tuna sandwich next to it—a small point but, well, fine dining is composed of small points, is it not?

Until next week, when I will demonstrate how to prepare a delicate Svenhard raisin snail in a toaster oven, without scorching the fennel seeds, this is once again your fast-food chef saying, *"Bon television!"*

THE SOUND OF ONE MIND, MINGLING

W ONDER IF IT's the right place. Doesn't seem to be anybody here yet. Think I'll sneak back to the car and read the paper until more people appear. Ah hah—there go two women. If I go in now, I can see who's coming and pounce, or depart early. The blonde taking tickets is gorgeous. An obvious plant. She's smiling at me but just wants ten bucks, not my body.

Guess I'll amble over to the bar and try to get lost in the huddle there. Need to hang onto a drink. Wonder if any of these waitresses are single. Feel better with a glass in hand. Look like I belong here.

Time to walk past the mirror and check out my hair and general adorability factor.

I look OK, though nothing to write home about. Feel like the new kid in class. Maybe if I comb my hair again I'll look more irresistible. Or if I stand sorta studlike, feet apart, right foot cocked . . . Say, there's a beauty! She's almost looking my way. Is that a half smile or just wishful thinking? I'll give her my Number 4 Roguish Grin and see what happens. She missed the entire smile. Seems she's smiling at someone behind me. Why does everyone else appear to know people? Not that I'd want to know them.

Time to walk across the room and lean against a pillar and survey people as they parade by. Like that sandy-haired woman with the crinkly blue eyes and sweet smile. I just may be in love. Lucky I got here early. Now if I can only maneuver into a smiling position. Why is she talking to that twerp who is coming on, as only twerps can. She seems indifferent, looking over at me, obviously signaling to be rescued. Be there in a minute, sweetheart! Hang on.

Maybe I'll get in line for food and stand next to some ravishing creature. Guess I won't. Line's too long, food looks rumpled and there are no ravishing creatures, just a floozy and two chubs, plus usual singles fare: day-old meatballs, cheese cubes, fritatta. Not worth standing in line for, much less eating. Knew I should have had dinner. Why do I always assume they'll serve real food?

Where's that lovely thing I was going to save a minute ago? Ah, there you are, me proud beauty! Now she's laughing. Curses. Waited too long; she's enjoying the twerp's jokes. Spies me out of the corner of her eye. Great twinkle. I'm definitely in love and will marry her if I can just pry her away from the twerp.

Can't think of how to get her attention. Twerp won't let her get a word in. She's nodding and smiling, but I know her heart's not in it. She awaits me to sidle up, swoop down and carry her off into the night.

Suppose beckoning her to come over is less than suave, yet a bold approach just might win her heart. She looks sensitive, like a woman who would appreciate a clever gesture. Better do something soon. I'll just slip into her line of vision, then sorta lean over extremely smoothly and say something bright and amusing, though am unsure of exact words. I'll think of something.

Now she's edging closer, sort of looking my way. This is it. She's gazing right at me, and I can't think. Here goes (not too snappy but it'll have to do): "You seem to know everybody!" "What's that?" My bride-to-be didn't even hear me and appears oblivious to my charms.

"I said, 'You seem to know everybody here.'" (Her smile vanishes. What have I done? Of the top 10 million openers, I choose No. 9,999,897.) "No, not really." She's hanging out the closed-for-tonight smile. I seem not to be doing overly well. Better pop some Clorets.

Who needs her? I'll do one more lap around and call it a night. Crowds are pouring in now, sweeping past in overheated swarm of bodies, people staring straight ahead, eyes aimed at some distant spot on the horizon. Nobody locks eyes for fear of seeming a needy case. What am I doing here? How low can a man sink!

Fritatta conga line now extends halfway to Reno—miles of strangers anxious for something to do that has more purpose than idling in place. There's that little bald guy with beady eyes who goes to everything—Pâté Breath. There's my ex-Rapunzel again, only now she's joking with two major jerks. One keeps squeezing her shoulder and shooting her little meaningful glances. How could I ever have been taken in by such an obvious tramp?

Can't stand this crowd. These are not my kind of people. Or maybe they are, and that's why I can't stand them. I'll leave in 15 minutes—well, no more than 30, as soon as I can work the other side of the room one last time . . .

Just as I figured—this is where the losers go to die. Wait! How is it possible this slim blonde has not yet been discovered? Lady luck, do your thing, babe.

Aforementioned pale beauty looks sublime from the side but I've been misled before by lovely three-quarter views. Better catch a full-face shot. Time for the ol' single-wing buttonhook—a casual stroll past, slow turn and nonchalant walk back. How awful of me; if she had a tire, I'd kick it. She looks OK—familiar even. I seem to know her. Could it be I took her out once and can't remember? The shame of it all.

That's it for tonight. I gave it my best shot and—but what's this? Someone smiling at me? How quaint. An actual cute person, too. I mumble something in return. We seem to be conversing; amazing but true. She's smiling like crazy. Wants to know my name. Shouts her name—Julie something. Great name, Julie. We fish for cards, laugh and repair to a corner table to move mouths and eyebrows over the music, as if conversing.

Have no idea what she's saying, but love how she looks saying it. Could be the start of something fun. Say, it's not a half-bad crowd, after all. Don't know why I was so surly earlier. Maybe I'll stick around a while and—hey, someone else just smiled. I'm on a roll. This is a lovely party, and I am one lovely guy.

THE LAUNDRY DATING WHIRL

HOWIE X, THE NEVER-SAY-DIE loser, has decided to give up on singles bars.

"I've been going to singles bars for nine years and never picked up anything but the check," says Howie. "I've got enough business cards to repaper my house, but whenever I call a woman, she can't remember me.

"Anyway, singles bars are passé, and I'm too old. Whenever I go into the Hard Rock, I feel like the dean of boys searching for uncontrolled substances."

Howie has begun to concentrate on laundromats, which he heard from his wild pal Leo is where it's happening. "I've found some incredibly foxy chicks at the Eezy Kleen on 38th Avenue," he reports. "It's a bit out of the way to get my clothes washed, but I'll try anything once."

"I've never spent much time around laundromats myself," I

said, "but I'm told museums are great pickup spots. The Frick Museum in New York—right under Vermeer's 'Mistress and Maid'—is reportedly a swinger's paradise."

Howie grumbled, "Like supermarkets, museums are vastly overrated. I used to go to the Museum of Modern Art until I couldn't bear the sight of another water lily. I am, however, quite an authority on Edward Hopper and the Ash Can School, not to mention the museum café brownies."

"Have you tried Thursday nights?" I asked. "They're free and are said to be veritable bacchanals, especially in the photo gallery, where I'm told anything can happen and usually does."

Howie frowned, "All the most intriguing women are too busy looking at the Karshes and Westins to notice me. They're actually interested in the art. It's pretty discouraging." He shook his head. "When I went to a Picasso exhibit, all I could think about was his sex life. His cubist stuff isn't bad, but the guy really made out like a bandit."

"It probably helps if you're Picasso," I said. "I imagine ol' Pablo never had to prowl the Louvre looking for girls. Say, how about art classes? I understand that's a terrific way to meet women."

"You were misinformed," said Howie. "It's all housewives starting second careers. The only available ones are the models. It's tough to walk up to a nude and ask if she'd like to join you after work for a drink. I may give the aquarium a shot. It's dark in there."

I asked Howie if he'd ever considered signing up for a ballet class. "It's the first thing I did when I got my divorce," he said. "I figured I'd be the only straight guy in class, and I was, but I forgot about the dancing part."

"Did it pay off as expected?"

"It was OK the first night, until I had to put on toe shoes and a leotard. The girls get pretty sweaty, which took an edge off the romantic aspect. Gelsey Kirkland they're not. It was more like Stillman's Gym."

"But it must be more promising than a laundromat on 38th Avenue," I insisted.

"Not so," winked Howie. "A laundromat is a basic meeting ground. First of all, it's *très intime*—just you and your boxer shorts and her and her teddies. You can tell right off who's single. You can also scope out their entire T-shirt collection, to see where they're at, politically and comically."

He added, "It's all very low key: unshaven, no makeup, with your basic morning face. You see each other at your absolute grungiest, and the lighting is so harsh that even Kelly McGillis would seem approachable."

Howie went on, "Then, too, you're thrown together because it's so dull. Nothing to read but torn up motorcycle magazines, baby sitter's phone numbers and lost-kitten fliers. Women are dying to talk, but usually the only other guy there is chatting to himself. I look great by comparison, especially in my fake jogging shorts."

"So you're really making the laundromat scene, eh?"

"I've met twice as many women folding towels on 38th Avenue as I ever did on Union Street. I'm known informally as the Warren Beatty of the spin-dry set."

"Sounds like you've found your true *métier* at last, Howie."

"I do OK, but it's nothing compared to the Versateller around the corner. Talk about a meat market."

TALES OF DELAY AND DELUSION

(The following episodes are true, except for names, places and minor details changed to protect everybody.)

GENE FELL in love with Lael while spending a week in Boston on business, but he left town before their romance could flower. He knew she was the love of his life, at last and forever. He wrote endless unanswered letters and made impassioned phone calls that Lael welcomed warmly but worriedly.

"It's doomed," she insisted. "We have other lives and live too far away. Forget me." Instead, he remembered her for six years until, one day, he had another reason to visit Boston. He called Lael and she sounded eager to see him; both were newly single. He was ecstatic. How would she look and seem to him? And he to her? At

the airport, she looked as beautiful and bewitching as the photo he had kept framed in his mind so long. That week, Lael went out of her way to be with him and he fell back in love with her. When, at long last, they made love, she was distant and sullen.

"What's wrong?" he said. "Was it disappointing?"

"No," she said. "It was too late."

"But I'm finally here," he said.

"You came when it was convenient, not when it counted," she said. "We waited too long." The next morning, Lael drove Gene to the airport, as before. They said good-by, as they had six years earlier. And as before, he went away.

Scott met Carol at a friend's dinner party, where they flirted outrageously until she left with her husband, Arthur. He asked to have lunch. "Sure," she said, "here's my card. Do call."

He did. Over spinach salad, Carol told Scott she wanted to have an affair. "But you're married," he said.

"I can work around it," she smiled. "Don't worry. It won't be a problem."

"I don't think it's such a good idea," Scott said.

"So what was all the flirting about?" she asked.

"I didn't think you'd take it seriously," he said.

"Well, I did, and now I want to sleep with you. Just once. I'll come by tomorrow night."

"Just once, though," he said, gravely. They made love and, as they got dressed, Carol said, "I guess I ought to tell you—I have herpes. In fact, so does Arthur, but I think it's a safe period now. Chances are you won't get it."

"That wasn't playing very fair," said Scott.

Carol looked at him in the mirror as she brushed her hair. "Tell me about it," she said.

Nat and Karen had been first-lovers in college but they separated soon afterward when he decided she wasn't bright enough for his literary ambitions.

Fourteen years later, when both were divorced, Karen walked into Nat's coffeehouse with a date and they chatted. He asked where she worked and the next day he called her.

They went out and spent the weekend at his apartment. The first night was wildly passionate. The following morning, they went for a late brunch and walked along Union Street, then came back to his house at 3:30, when he felt their conversation waning.

"Well, it's been wonderful," said Nat.

"I suppose I should get back," she said. "It's a long drive . . ." When he said nothing, Karen asked, "Tell me just one thing before I leave, Nat—what went wrong?"

"I never knew," he said, "and I've wondered about it for fourteen years."

"I don't mean then," Karen said. "I mean now. Today. You lost interest all over again, I could tell. You still don't think I'm smart enough."

"Don't be silly," he said. "It's been wonderful, us getting back together. I loved it."

"You only love the idea of us. It appeals to your romantic fantasies, but you're bored with the real us. Like before." Nat said nothing. Karen smiled, "It's OK, I can handle it now. I'm all grown up, if you hadn't noticed. And I also know I'm smart enough—for me."

"Too smart in a way," he said as tenderly as possible. He walked Karen to her car, kissed her good-by and said, "I hope we see each other again."

"I see you fine," she said. "I just wish you saw me. You have to focus harder, Nat. Here I am. *Look*."

THE MARRIED MAFIA

Is it just my old paranoia kicking up again or do newlyweds purposely exclude old single friends from their lives, comfortable only with their own kind?

In his dress-and-tell book, Prince Charles' valet wrote that when the boss got married, "certain friends had to go, because they just didn't fit in anymore."

Granted, Chuck and Di are a rather special case, but it does often seem that, just as when a couple splits up and stops seeing their old married friends, when two people marry they cut their single chums loose.

Probably it's all imagined but, in the words of the royal valet, maybe we just don't fit in. Single men, far from being in great demand at dinner parties as "extra gentlemen," are more like fifth wheels. A single woman in a crowd of couples, if she's invited at all, feels like a mateless sock.

Or it may be that couples feel obliged to see only couples (the Ark Syndrome) when they might prefer to mix it up with their rough-and-tumble single cronies.

Many couples become small, family-run corporations. Others try to see their old single friends alone rather than bore a spouse with old jokes and war stories from the unwedded front lines. Some women can't stand a man's premarital buddies; her old girlfriends drive him nuts.

There is also a presumption among couples that single men are far too busy to be interested in a bunch of old married folks when, in fact, seasoned married people are a refreshing change from the usual old singles gang.

It's great to have a night off from stewing over commitment and biological clocks, to cease talking about relationship theory and observe it in practice. I regard married couples as intriguing lab specimens.

At the same time, married people treat us differently because of our peculiar condition. We're like someone who's ailing. To couples, a single person is not quite well, not quite an entire person.

Maybe married people just feel uneasy around the unmarried, considering us unworthy of being allowed into their exclusive social set, where only two can play. We have to earn our way in by proving our pairworthiness, like being tapped for a fraternity. As soon as you announce you're engaged—or even just going with someone—married people seem happier to see you again. You're back safely from the Other Side.

I do it rarely, but double-dating with married people is a very strange concept, especially if the married pair drive, which they tend to insist upon. In the back seat, I feel like I'm being taken to the prom by my parents, even if I'm older than the married people.

I hate to think so, but I suspect it's because, in a group of mixed doubles, the married pair automatically become the grownups and the single people the kids. The marrieds decide where to eat, give *their* name at the restaurant and insist on paying.

To me, it's married people who are the rare birds, especially if they've been married more than ten years. They've become objects of reverence, like the elderly in Asia, merely for their longevity.

In years to come, people who have been married twenty years will become eligible for some sort of government pension, or perhaps a foundation grant from Gerber's, Pampers and the builders of two-story homes.

There is, in fact, a new book out on married people who have stayed together and how they did it. I see a TV show in it: "Ladies and gentlemen, Mr. and Mrs. Geller have been living under one roof for seventeen years! *That's Incredible!!*"

It feels strange when people your age have been married as long as your parents were when you were a kid; fifteen years is a golden anniversary. Old married couples are modern curiosities. Pretty soon anyone married for thirty years will go on tour.

HALF A LOAF IS BETTER THAN ONE

A S YET ANOTHER example of my untapped entrepreneurial instincts, I am proposing a grocery store that caters exclusively to single people. I have everything figured out but the name: Singleway? Solo Foods? I like *Shop-for-One*.

To guard against spoilage, the single person's arch enemy, we plan to offer various house brands, items such as Bread-for-One— a loaf of ten slices with a shelf life of two months; Lettuce-for-One,

 consisting of half a head; and, instead of an ungainly Sara Lee tin, bitesize pieces of Cake McNuggets.

Efficiency aside, this grocery should help people take off weight. Left alone, singles eat everything in sight, feeling a need to polish off all leftovers, hungry or no, so as not to waste anything.

Most singles' refrigerators are filled with fifteen or twenty covered dishes containing the last ninth of a can of chili, four slices of canned peaches, five Niblets, half a spoonful of apple sauce—much of it never consumed or even looked at again. It sits there until declared dead, then is quickly flung in a Baggie with both eyes shut.

At Shop-for-One, we will package leftovers in attractive plastic containers, with amusing sayings on the side, or perhaps operate a Leftovers Exchange, a sort of garage sale for second-hand food.

We'll only build express lanes at Shop-for-One, to serve you better, with one super-express lane (two items or less). Anyone buying more than nine items must go around twice or find a regular grocery.

Shop-for-One should become a popular singles meeting ground, replacing passé bars and health spas, making it unnecessary to spin your wheels at the local Safeway, wondering who is and is not married.

Half of Shop-for-One will be devoted to frozen foods of all kinds, with a research and development division to invent frozen blackened redfish and broiled sea bass with dill sauce, perhaps even complete Thanksgiving dinners that may be popped in a microwave. TV meals will be wrapped discreetly in brown paper to disguise their identity.

We'll sell three-packs of beer and pre-separate bananas from bunches so as not to humiliate people forced to buy a single banana. Half avocados will be available, also tuna by the short ton, 500 tins per carton; peanut butter will come in 50-pound economy-size jars.

Shop-for-One shall feature a clothing department, where socks are sold singly to match existing loners—with a Press 'n' Shop counter to allow people to drop off a pair of pants or a blouse upon entering and pick them up on the way out, crisply creased.

Our Shop-for-One produce department will be staffed with attractive female clerks to explain the identities and purposes of obscure melons and beans, give advice on candying yams and gutting artichokes, and to discuss the many uses of buffalo mozzarella.

Likewise, Shop-for-One's butcher counter will include a round-the-clock information booth where highly trained experts will be on hand at all hours to explain the difference between a loin and a rump roast.

There will be a sushi bar, a wine bar and a juice bar for happy-hour shoppers who want to unwind before heading home to a sinkful of week-old dishes. After shopping, customers can pop in for a quick pick-me-up, perhaps striking up a conversation with a comely unattached neighbor:

"Hi, there. Buy you another S&W peach nectar?"

"I'm afraid I—"

"I'm a cranapple guy myself. Say, maybe we could pop over to my place around the corner for a twilight cap. I just picked up some of this vintage *crème fraîche* and a box of Carr's water crackers. You up for it?"

"I don't do crackers and cheese with strangers. Besides, I have to get this sourdough pizza in the oven before it thaws."

"Yum-yum! Look, I'm usually here after work. Maybe we can split a barbecued chicken sometime."

"Gee, I'd like that."

NOBODY HERE BUT US STOOLS

I T'S BEEN MY experience, after an extensive study of 438 singles bars, that nobody goes to a singles bar on purpose.

Oh, they may *be* there but they don't *go* there. The bar just kind of grew up around them, like the ferns.

If you meet someone in a singles bar, it's a fluke. They wandered in by accident, or they had heard about this place and thought they'd just sorta check it out for a moment. Or their friend is a waitress and they stopped in to say hi.

As many as seven out of ten singles are from out of town. Just blew in from Portland and decided to drop by to use the cigarette machine, the rest room, the juke box.

People who admit to coming directly from work are there on serious business, which rarely has to do with meeting other people. Oh, they'll talk to other people if it can't be helped, but they're not really there to, you know, socialize.

Everyone you meet at singles bars disapproves of them. Many were dragged in, bound and gagged; most are there under duress. Some come for "business contacts."

The majority of people who don't go to singles bars are women. In surveying 1,622 people at singles bars throughout the city, I uncovered two men who claimed to be there looking for women. No women were there to find men, however. A few times, I even had to define the word "man."

"Oh, that!" one woman said, slapping her forehead. "You mean guys, hunks, studs, fellows, male individuals."

"That's the general concept," I said.

The purpose of singles bars, I quickly learned, is to meet old friends. I always assumed that all those people you see at such places are there to meet new people. Not true.

This is how I discovered the Society of Friends, which is un-affiliated with the Quakers. The Society of Friends is made up of people who are meeting the people you meet at singles bars. One such "friend" said he spends about four nights a week meeting people at singles bars. "It's demanding work," he says. "I have to meet about 2,000 people a night."

Most of the women I met were on their way to dinner with A Friend. Not all, however. Many were not having dinner and were on their way to a movie, where they would be meeting A Friend.

Women who weren't meeting Friends had work to do and were on their way home. Some carried large pouches under their arms, crammed with manila folders.

Many women, not wanting to be mistaken for common singles, had brought along entire filing cabinets, which added to the bar crush. None of them, oddly, were there for the purpose of meeting strangers, a practice they all despised, to a woman.

Singles bars, contrary to popular belief, are not pickup joints. Nobody has ever been inside one more than once. Some 98.8 percent of the people at a singles bar are there for the first time. The other 1.2 percent are there for dinner. "The food here's really quite good," all agree.

Many people go to singles bars to "people watch," a favorite of women under 25, who haven't seen a lot of people before. "This is a great place to watch people!" one stewardess said. "I'm a big people watcher."

I pointed out that airports and department stores are fun watching places, too, both filled with people, many more than you find at a singles bar. I suggested she check out Macy's sometime. "Great place to people watch," I said.

I saw she was impressed. "Thanks for the tip," she said, hopping off a stool. "So long. I think I see my friend over there."

HOW DO I LOVE THEE? LET ME EVADE THE WAYS

S O FAR AS I know, none of the major (or even desktop) greet-
ing card companies has come to grips with the problems of
modern entanglements, cards for people who care enough to
send their second best.

We have lacy valentines, funny valentines, scented and quilted
valentines, sexy and even sleazy valentines. What we do not have
is singles valentines.

The reason, of course, is that modern romance is so complex
and confused that it really requires a Henry James, F. Scott Fitzgerald or John Updike to express just the proper emotional shad-
ings—off-red. The Hallmark people obviously aren't up to the job;
they still deal in devoted, everlasting-type love, which, it often appears, went out some time ago.

Why, for instance, is there no card for someone who has just
had a baby by you out of wedlock? What do you send someone you
no longer go with but remain fond of? Where is a sentiment to express the subtle degrees of non-commitment felt by a man for a
woman he adores but isn't going to marry?

These are delicate poetic questions, and at $1 per card, valen-
tine shoppers have a right to expect more than a talking
hippopotamus.

In the past, one was either in love or one was not in love, which
made it a snap. Now, of course, the very word "love" is so multi-
faceted, overdone and just plain suspect that it can only be used
under the most carefully circumscribed conditions.

What we need is a line of valentines for insecure lovers. There's
an urgent need for a valentine to express the fear of commitment
toward someone you could love with certain conditions attached,
something along the lines of:

"I definitely love you/Except on weekends/When I need to be by myself/Which isn't to say I don't love you then/But that I have other priorities/Which I know you understand/But that I wanted to spell out just in case."

This sort of thing, in blank verse, gets to the heart of so many modern blank feelings.

Where is a card you can send to a former lover who found someone else but is miserable and for whom you still have a certain affection? Is there a poet working who can put *that* into tender verse?

The list of neglected lovers is endless: No cards for the closet gay; none for the busy bisexual, the nymphomaniac or your favorite tramp; no sweet nothings that delineate the nuances of feeling one has for the woman in the next apartment, for the boss' daughter or your ex-girlfriend's married niece, for that winsome bank teller or dental hygienist in your life.

Alas, no cards for the amicably divorced who still see their ex-spouses for fun; no frilly hearts for older women to give young studs; no rhymes for sugar daddies to send to the gold-diggers of their dreams; no tender lines for cheating married lovers to slip each other; no adoring cards for some flirty Baskin-Robins clerk or a nubile second cousin you fantasize about.

There are songs, but no cards, for unrequited lovers—or, even more delicate, for someone who's in love with *you* but whom you only like as a friend. And where is a nice (but not too nice) card to give your mate during a separation, a quandary I once found myself in. No card, either, for the marriage counselor you're mad for.

I've never seen a card to send someone you're half in love with, the major unfilled category. If the verse is too torrid, you're going to look idiotic and blow it; if it's too trivial, you won't be taken seriously, which is worse.

Most cards are too lovey-dovey or too flip, which doesn't matter on birthdays or anniversaries, but St. Valentine's Day is serious business, and you can't be half a degree off. If a card isn't on the nose, it's not worth the recycled paper it's written on.

Today's cards say too much or too little. The funny ones are too funny, the cute ones too cute, the clever ones not as clever as they think. They all just miss.

Maybe the best cards were those funny looking, slightly smudged, handmade jobs you did as a passionate kid and covertly stuck in a box on the teacher's desk. They took days to make and were crafted of stiff red paper, paste and doilies, and then coyly signed in crayon, "*With Love, From Me*" or "*Guess Who??*"

St. Valentine's Day is still too important to be left to the professionals.

EX-SWINGER IN SLUMP

I RAN INTO my favorite swinging bachelor, Phil Lander, the other night at Mulhern's and, of all things, he was drinking alone at the bar.

"What's wrong, Phil?" I asked him, noting a gloomy look on his usually animated face. "Where's your bevy of beguiling beauties?"

"I've had to cut back severely on my sexual activity," he said, stirring a desultory gin and tonic.

"Ah, of course," I said. "Very wise idea. It's a real health risk."

"Oh, that's not the reason," he said. "I'm careful. No, the main problem is that I can't get anywhere with women anymore. I've lost it."

"Too old?"

"Hey, I'm only 38. Gimme a break. No, the problem is that I don't speak their language."

"But you've always been at ease with women. Everything you said sent them into peals of laughter."

"Not anymore. In the old days, I could regale a woman with my funny stories or wow her with my knowledge of the A's pitching staff and the '49ers defensive team. I could impress her with my insights on the turbo-power of the new cars.

"If that failed, I could dazzle her with my high-powered job that takes me to exotic locales or charm her with my financial acumen. As a last resort, I could wow her with my athletic prowess."

"So?"

"So every woman I meet now knows better jokes, can more astutely discuss Joe Montana's arm, drives a sleeker sportscar, travels more and can whip me at tennis, run rings around me and bench press 150 pounds."

"How discouraging for you."

"I believe the word is humiliating. Before, I had nothing in common with the women I met, and now I have too much in common."

"How is this bad?"

"Women aren't interested in my fascinating lifestyle. Their lives are twice as fascinating and they're not snowed by all that. At first, it was sort of fun comparing money-market portfolios . . ."

"I guess you can't build a relationship on that," I noted.

"You can't even start one. There's no more thrill of the unknown when you meet a woman at a singles joint."

"She's heard it all, eh?"

Phil added, "What's worse, I now have to sit there politely and listen to all of her stories about life in the executive suite—what a drag. I used to think it was pretty exciting stuff, when they were my stories. When I hear them coming back at me, I check out."

I gnawed a pretzel and nodded.

"If I meet one more woman lawyer or a chick who sells software, I'm going to get married. It's bad enough that men have nothing to talk about but their careers, but you expect more from women. Boy, I'd love to meet a teacher, a nurse or a waitress—just for an adventure!"

"The men have pretty well moved into those areas," I said.

Phil went on: "In the early '80s, men were able to make their life sound incredibly exciting, but women realize what a lot of hogwash it is. They always sort of sensed it; now they know it."

"How do you beguile a woman nowadays?" I wondered.

"Don't ask me," he shrugged. "Lately, I've tried everything—my whole arsenal of formerly guaranteed mesmerizing stories from the fascinating world of business and commerce—but all I get from women is a glazed look."

"Just not interested, eh?"

"Even if they are, they're much too tired to go out. It's all they can do to shlep themselves in here with their bulging attaché cases. Just when I think I'm doing well enough to propose dinner, they say they've got to catch an early plane the next morning for Tokyo but will call me when they get back."

"And?"

"They give me their card and that's the last I ever hear from them. You know women."

WHEN I'M 64, YOU'LL LOVE ME

SINGLE MEN ARE SAID to die earlier than married guys, whereas single women live longer but go crazy earlier. Clearly, this is part of a scientific campaign to scare me into marriage. Sorry, I'm not buying it.

When these grisly statistics are cited, there is always "medical evidence," but it wouldn't stand up in a court of law. Much of this evidence, I suspect, is prepared by married people, chortling to themselves.

One classic argument, frequently expressed by married women, is: "What are you going to do when you get old and sick?"

I do think about this, but I have a foolproof plan: When and if I get old (medical evidence suggests a 72 percent likelihood), I shall simply get married. This will halt the aging process and, I am sure, add years to my life.

Were I to marry today, I would use up all the rejuvenating benefits by the time I was 80. Why waste it on me now?

"But who's going to *want* you when you're old and sick?" is the usual rude rejoinder.

Well, I've thought about that, too, and have it all worked out. I expect to be this incredibly charming old guy, with a twinkle in my eye and an irresistible fund of knowledge, which I shall impart at the drop of a hat—but not so I bore people, naturally. (If nobody has a hat, I will drop one of my own.)

I expect to have plenty of wise things to say, endless anecdotes and a lovable manner that women of all ages will find irresistible, somewhat more than they do now.

Anyone who *doesn't* find me irresistible shall be shown the door, and fast. I won't have time for the disinterested, as I will not suffer fools gladly, unless they're rather cute fools; one can't be too inflexible.

When I get old, I intend to be witty, dapper and wise, a blend of George Burns, Don Ameche and the late William O. Douglas—catnip to young girls is the general plan. These young things will want to help me across the street and even show me home, to make sure I arrive safely.

I may adopt a monocle (this part hasn't quite been worked out yet), carry a gold-tipped cane and perhaps even grow some sort of beard—a Van Dyke or mutton-chops. This will make me at least appear fascinating, should I fail in that department.

If I don't already have one, I may affect a slight limp, to add to my overall mystique. I'll say I got it during the Spanish Civil War, when I served with Hemingway and Dos Passos as an ambulance driver.

I expect I'll join a club, something I've long avoided, so I can sink into a huge leather armchair and fall asleep reading the newspaper—much as I do now, only without a waiter to shake me awake with a glass of sherry. I may even take up drinking sherry.

Unlike many older people, I won't have to worry why my kids don't ever call or visit, saving me much needless anxiety that sends parents to an early grave. Should I feel an overwhelming need for ungrateful children, I'll visit some of my friends' kids and badger them into calling me.

What I would like, however, is a couple of grandchildren to sit at my knee and listen to all my stories. I expect to have some stories by the time I'm older; if not, there's no need for grandchildren. Actually, I tell terrible stories and would be a major washout as a grandfather. I'd have to purchase some outside anecdotes.

My pockets will be stuffed with candy, of course, so that children will flock to me, stories or no stories, like beloved old Mr. Drosselmeyer in *The Nutcracker*, my general working model of how I expect to be received.

Being an old guy without any stories could be embarrassing. The children would just sit there waiting for a fascinating tale of my youth, such as when I stowed away on a tramp steamer from Omsk.

Instead, all I'd have would be a couple of thin anecdotes about when I went to New York as a young man to seek my fortune, only to return to California, penniless, a year later. I doubt if that would keep too many ten-year-olds at my knee; frankly, I'm pretty sick of it myself.

PLATO, LET'S JUST BE FRIENDS

Last week at the Balboa Café, I ran into Guy Solo, an old bachelor pal, who was terribly distraught.

"Why the long face?" I asked.

"It seems that every other woman I take out these days wants to be my friend," he said. "What did I do?"

"Well, it happens," I said. "You must learn to expect an occasional friendship. It can't be helped."

"But I've got enough friends. I want romance."

"Romance is not in the cards with these women?"

"God only knows. Some just aren't interested, and others are 'involved' but still go out. It's maddening. They're about two-thirds single."

"It's hard to be a little bit single," I said. "I don't know how they do it."

Guy said, "It's reverse cheating. Either you're available or you're not. They may as well be married. We have a good time as long as I'm indifferent. If I get interested, they draw the line. I can sense when the Friend Speech is coming. Their voice drops, they fold their hands and look like a doctor explaining I have a month to live: 'I think we have to talk about something, Guy. I like you a *lot* but, well, I *am* sort of seeing someone right now.'"

I suggested that perhaps some women just put it this way to be kind, if you're not their type.

"I know," he said. "One woman didn't tell me until our sixth date that she had a lover, which explained allthose lingering good-

night smiles. Women with lovers should wear something to signal their semi-attached status."

He added, "Usually, the better friends I become with a woman, the more intrigued I get, and the more frustrated. Women are capable of platonic affairs but with men it's all or nothing."

"And I always thought women were the all-or-nothing species," I said. "Men are such romantics, really. Shaw was right. Women are the practical, hardheaded ones."

Guy shook his head. "Women feel that if you sleep with someone, you're in love. These are the same people who say sex is just part of a relationship."

"Until it's with someone else," I said. "Then it means you must be in love. So tell me, why can't you go out with a woman and just talk?"

"I don't want to be a friend object," said Guy. "I feel used. I'm sick of being kept on a string until a woman feels in the mood for a little chat."

"Like a piece of conversational meat," I added. "Who wants to be a faceless man that a woman feels she can get whatever she wants from—companionship, sharing—only to be cast aside when she's had her way?"

"Oh, they can be cruel!" he said, bitterly. "All these female chums only want you for one thing—closeness. They're just in it for your unique male perspective."

"Yep," I said, "lady friends are unfeeling monsters. How do you ward off their non-sexual advances?"

"Usually I agree to remain friends, certain that eventually my natural charm will make me irresistible."

"Does it?" I asked him.

"What happens is, if I can maintain the charade long enough, we *do* end up friends—just about the time she's breaking up. If you can wait out some of these friendships, it pays off. Except by then I know so much about them that I've lost all romantic interest."

I added, "And if you should get mad, it makes you seem like a sexist pig, with no interest in their mind."

Guy said, "You got it. I'll do anything not to seem like a sexist pig, so I always say, 'Sure, sure, I understand. We'll be friends for life. You busy Saturday?'"

"A major tactical error. Platonic dates are never available on weekends. You can't mention weekends, travel or anything with even the vaguest sexual overtones." Then I asked him, "Don't you have any women friends that you have no romantic interest in?"

"Just those I used to be in love with. When all the passion burns away, I'm usually left with a friend."

"Ex-lovers make great pals," I agreed.

"Exactly," said Guy. "Which is why I don't need any new ones. They'll like you and leave you."

THE RISE AND FALL OF SEX

SEX HAS HAD its ups and downs since I was a boy. First, there wasn't enough sex. This occurred right at the time I was widely thought to be sowing my wild oats. My wild oats, warehouses and silos full of them, awaited sowing. After that, there was too much sex around. Sex was rampant, available for a mere tip of the hat. This happened when my oats had been domesticated and I was no longer able to take advantage of it.

Now that I'm again single, there is less sex each day, with predictions that premarital sex has just about had it. Marriage is where all the action is.

This new development in sexual relations comes as a bitter jolt to people who, while married, heard rumors of more sex on the outside than a body could handle. In the '70s and early '80s, unmarried folks were dropping from exhaustion. All you had to do was stand in a singles bar, or even at a salad bar, and all these lovely women would sidle over and whisper, "If you want anything, just whistle." Often, even whistling was unnecessary.

Four hours after I was divorced, the sexual revolution ground to a halt. Word got out, apparently, that a lunatic was loose and that definite curbs would have to be put on the sexual revolution, to protect women and girls yet unborn.

Reports began filtering in from the trenches that women were changing their minds. Again. They no longer felt a need to go to bed with a man just to, you know, experiment, even if the pill and Cosmo had freed them from any such prissy constraints. They were having second thoughts; they were being more discreet. I was just in time for the Discreet Sex Revolution.

To make things worse, marriage got trendy; it was on all the magazine covers and young people (i.e., young female people) decided that marriage was what they wanted, not random sex; sex for sex's sake was passé. Weddings were back, along with TGIF parties and '57 Pontiacs. Women now wanted that special guy. I was just in time for the Special Guy Revolution.

Due to herpes, chlamydia, AIDS, etc., people grew cautious, afraid of the consequences, just like when I was in sexual knickers. No more French kissing after 10 P.M. No more "casual sex." Sex must have serious long term aims. Now I'm in time for the Non-Casual Sex Revolution.

All agree that the new attitude toward sex is wise and finally may put sex in its proper perspective, so I'm also in time for the Sex-in-Its-Proper-Perspective Revolution.

The entire tenor of dating is undergoing vast changes. Without sex to look forward to, whatever will we all do after dinner and an Australian movie?

He: It's been real nice, Sue (leans forward to kiss).

She: Look, Ralph, it isn't that I'm not *terribly* attracted to you, and would love to jump in the sack, but our block is under quarantine through July.

He: Hey, it's OK. I have to get up early tomorrow anyway. The fumigators are coming at 7:30 . . . I know—let's go to my place and . . .

She: Are you out of your *mind*? Have you already forgotten what you told me—that you once dated a woman who had roomed with a woman who had lived in Miami and once dated a part-Haitian hair stylist?

He: I know, I know. I didn't have anything intimate in mind. I just thought I could show you my etchings.

She: Very amusing (rolls eyes).

He: But I actually *have* etchings, and they're pretty doggone erotic—one even shows people actually kissing on the lips and stuff, like in the old days. I'll behave.

She: I think not, Ralph. Let's call it a night, OK? It's late, and if I don't sign in by midnight, I'll be locked out again. Twice in one month and I lose my lease.

HAVE A BABY (HAVE TWO, THEY'RE SMALL)

MY TICKET FAILED to arrive for the Blue & Pink Ball, the spring cotillion given by Parents Without Parsons, women in their thirties looking for eligible fathers. So I called on the group's founder, Esther Prynn.

"We're the women whose biological clock says six minutes to midnight and who want a baby without benefit of clergy," explained Esther. Her Parents Without Parsons is a new support group for women who, in less enlightened times, were scorned and burned at the stake.

"We used to call it having a kid out of wedlock," I said.

"Get with it, Mister. This is the era of the celebrity bastard. All your best people are having babies illegitimately—people like Jessica and Sam and Mick and Jerry. It's *très chic*.

"Oh," I said, "it's become positively dear. People magazine is full of famous adoring papas dandling their illegit kids."

The only men invited to the Blue & Pink Ball are prospective fathers with good breeding and genetic makeup. "It's a pretty exclusive shindig," she said.

"Not unlike the Nazi party," I said. "Quite a ritual."

"Don't be wise," huffed Esther. "It's just a progressive dating service. Women who want to meet eligible dads put on their sexiest duds and take the man they'd most like to have a baby by."

"So how do *I* get invited?"

"Pass a rigorous physical," she explained. "Names of men who make the final cut are tossed into a barrel. Whoever draws your genetic code is your, ah, 'date.'"

"Suppose they don't like the cut of my genes?"

"Your code is traded to another woman."

"Sounds like the NFL draft."

Esther smiled, "We think of it as a church social, without the church. We're actually preserving the future of mankind—babykind, anyway."

"How pro-life of you. Is Mrs. Schlafley behind this?"

"Not yet," said Esther. "The point is, with marriage so difficult, and men so impossible, this is the only way for many good women to become moms."

"Whatever became of Zero Population Growth? In 1975, that was every forward-thinking woman's top priority."

"We're 15 years older," she said.

"I'm glad kids are politically correct. In 1975, people marched against population explosion, protesting women as baby machines, refusing to bring generations never-to-be-born into a world ravaged by hunger and nuclear uncertainty. What became of all that?"

"It's just that babies are *so* cute," she dimpled.

"Yeah, but don't they need fathers around?"

"Fathers get in the way, assuming they're around at all. Our ideal donor dad gets lost as soon as possible. We encourage men to leave once they've done the right thing by the mother and made her an honest woman."

"I thought such men were the scum of the earth!"

"We now believe men are good for only one thing."

"What about all the guys who'd love to meet a nice girl, settle down and have kids the old-fashioned way?"

"Well, today anything's possible. We're not against cohabitation—if the man makes a fuss—but we wish he'd visit a maiden aunt or go to Europe. We have our careers. Who needs a guy who'll just hold us back?"

I asked Esther to wangle me an invite to the Blue & Pink Ball. "If I let *you* in," she said, "we'll have to let in all sorts of undesirables who will dance but won't mate."

"Is there a press list?" I said. "I have credentials. No diseases, no mental illness to speak of, all my own hair."

"Do you need to wear corrective lenses at night?"

"You mean for driving?"

"Not exactly. Can you see in the dark? It's crucial."

"Hey, I've got eyes like a cat."

"Good teeth? I notice a gap. How's your bite?" I bit down on her arm. "Seems firm for a white male of your age. Do you have any photos of yourself in a swimsuit?" I pulled out a snapshot. "These aren't recent," she frowned.

"I don't swim now. That was in '83. I look the same."

Esther frowned. "I'll need your SATs, and have you any special talents? Can you sing, play the harp, sew, split an atom, make a fortune, that sort of thing?"

When I said no, Esther suggested a new male support group that I have since joined, Bachelors Without Babies.

WHAT'S YOUR FLIRTING SIGN?

AFTER READING AN interview with Cynthia Kline, who teaches an actual course in "How to Flirt," I decided to take her advice and sashayed into a local single's hangout last Friday night at happy hour to test some of her theories.

I spotted a fabulous looking creature at the bar stroking her long, honey colored hair. What luck! Ms. Kline claims that women who run their hands through their hair, or dare to comb it in front of you, are definitely "interested."

I sidled over, winked and mumbled, "Hello, sweetheart. Only a fool would fail to notice the way you're flashing your hair around. Mind if I move into your personal space?"

She shrugged. I let it be known that, if she cared, she might touch me anywhere on my person—except the crotch, which, according to Ms. Kline, is the one area considered by men to be off limits for flirting.

Some men maybe. Me, I like a woman who's not afraid to show interest. Nothing like a harmless squeeze to let a guy know you take a fancy to him.

Cynthia Kline says most men can't tell when a woman is giving obvious signals. This babe was flashing signals like O'Hare Airport. She licked her lips, blinked and stirred her drink in a counterclockwise motion—a veritable Salome.

At one point, she even touched her ear, which means only one thing, says Kline. I leaned forward, invading her space again, and whispered, "I'm free right now." She knitted her brow (a telltale sign), shifted her body weight (slut!) and flounced out. I'd misread her.

In a corner, I noticed a cute redhead all by herself and, after inquiring if she came here often, I gently touched her between the elbow and wrist, said by Kline to be a provocative sign.

She stroked her chin—a classic come-on—and said, echoing Ms. Kline, "You've just entered the two-foot 'bubble' surrounding my body, generally considered in North America to be personal space."

"Sorry if I seem forward," I said, "but I'm from Venezuela, and down there it's only 18 inches."

She bristled and said, "Maybe some Latin bimbo will buy that, but I wasn't born yesterday." She looked up Venezuela in her Filofax. "It says here that the 'personal bubble' around a woman is four feet in Caracas. Sorry, buster."

I smiled, acknowledged by flirting expert Kline to be "a sign of friendliness and encouragement." She winked at the man on her left, which I intuited as a possible indication of non-receptiveness. I reread Kline's article closely.

I then approached a lanky brunette and touched her gently about the forearm, spilling her drink in her lap.

Happily, she was svelte and tall, which played into my hands perfectly. Kline says that, should I meet such a woman, a good way to flirt might be to tease by calling her "Slim."

"How's the weather up there, Slim?" I said roguishly.

She was all over me. "You big tease!" she said, brushing her hair in rapid strokes and toying with her key ring, two sure flirtatious signs, according to Ms. K.

"You have a cute way of toying with your key ring," I said. She ran her hand down her thigh and then over her buttocks, "two unconscious erotic gestures," claims Kline.

I sensed Slim was excited but I wasn't sure until she displayed an open palm, indicating "the woman is open to your advances." Grabbing her, I said, "I want your palm."

She blushed and said, "I hope you don't think I'm in the habit of opening my hand 10 minutes after I meet someone. Usually, it takes me at least 45 minutes. I like to know a guy first."

"Don't be silly," I said. "I respect a frank, open woman. I'll show you my palm if you show me yours." One sign led to another and she invited me up to her place. We flirted on the rug until 2 A.M.

"I think you'd better go," she finally gasped, straightening her key ring.

"Call you Monday," I said. "I'd like to decipher you again."

PARTYING IS
SUCH SWEET SORROW

A MARRIED FRIEND recently made a crack to the effect that I hadn't invited her and her husband to dinner. This was in response to my own injured retort at not being invited to a recent dinner of theirs.

"You never have *us*," I believe was her exact phrasing. "I never have anyone," I shot back, but it failed to mollify her. Being single is my excuse for not entertaining. It's not because I don't cook. I don't cook because I don't have enough napkins. Also, it makes me crazy.

I could learn to cook, I suppose, but this would require more years than I have to spare just now. I got a gift certificate for a cooking class from this very woman, who is determined to turn me into Wolfgang Puck.

When I entertain, I grow very grumpy if, the day before, anyone cancels. It undoes me. I never cancelled a meal in my life. Recently, I co-hosted a birthday dinner and, midway through the onion soup, a couple called to say they couldn't make it. Rather, someone called them, wondering if they needed directions. The dinner had slipped their minds. I also never forgot a meal in my life.

Nobody RSVPs on time. People who do RSVP call later to say they can't make it after all; some nonsense about a sick child. Those who do make it, come an hour late as the cheese sweats. By dinner, I'm in tears.

There's always one guest who got the day mixed up and has another party, so he can't arrive until after dinner, and somebody always calls to ask if he can bring a college friend who's in town.

I have given what I call "desserts" or "coffees," which isn't as difficult as a four-course meal but you get almost as much credit. I'm taking it a course at a time. I can handle hors d'oeuvres; next year, perhaps I'll attempt appetizers. By the time I'm 55, I may try a simple soup, and, when I'm 60, concoct an entire entree. What you need are people who know what they're doing. These people are called women.

I am, however, quite proficient at buying cake and ice cream, an undervalued talent rife with unforeseen problems. I also make a respectable pot of coffee, but there's more to coffee than meets the eye. You must cope with people who drink tea (just to rattle me); some want decaf, and others demand Sweet 'n' Low and low-fat milk instead of cream. Don't forget dessert forks. And napkins—cloth ones, with actual creases.

If it weren't for napkins, I'd be a fabulous host, but I don't own enough napkins of the same design, and you don't dare give people assorted napkins. They'll leave early, grousing on the way home what a crummy party it was, "Can you imagine that guy having the gall to mix yellow and red napkins!"

Once I did "entertain," to stretch the term somewhat. It amounted to ordering four extra-large pizzas, but I did personally select the cole slaw, potato salad and cake, and I made the coffee. It was an exhausting effort.

It sounded like a snap, "having a few people in for pizza," but the details got me down. Simple things, like chairs. There are never enough chairs, unless guests juggle plates on their laps, which won't work because they can't talk and watch TV (this was an Oscars party), and if they're all in the same room there won't be enough space for everyone to see the screen.

Thinking ahead, I got an extra TV set, one for the study and one for the front room, prompting everyone to crowd into the front room, nicely ruining my plan. Crowd control is a major part of home entertaining.

"When should we order the pizza?" is the sort of question that still stumps the U.N. General Assembly. Do you order pizza when people arrive, when the show starts, during a commercial or when the foreign short-subject award is being given out?

I also had to determine what sort of drinks would be appropriate—soda, beer, wine, mineral water, all this in addition to coffee, tea, decaf, etc. ("Got any juice?") The potato salad was easy; I shoveled it onto a big plate. I advise potato salad for all parties.

Simply ordering pizza for ten is enough to convince me I'm not cut out for entertaining on even the most primitive level. Subsidiary problems include: Which pizza parlor to call? What kind of pizza to order? How big?

By the time the pizza guy arrived (after 45 minutes of me frantically peering through the blinds), I couldn't eat; my stomach was in knots. I may throw a party sometime this year, but no more pizza. Too tricky. I'd like to do something simpler, like maybe ask a few people in for toast and cornflakes. Bring Your Own Napkins.

LIVING TOGETHER— A FLING OF THE PAST

MARRIAGE IS IN. Marriage is back. Marriage is on the march. There's every indication that marriage has caught on again, especially with motherhood making such a nice little comeback of its own.

This is terrific news for single people, for it could put an end to that foggy state of suspended animation: Living Together, which is not quite living and not quite together.

Living Together, you'll recall, was once going to solve the domestic blues (no more sticky divorces, no more sticky children), but it seems to have lost much of its old promise and all of its former luster. Premarital sex slowly evolved into premarital sox.

For years, single people were allied against the common foe— wedlock—until Living Together put a serious dent into singledom. Suddenly, you didn't know who was available and who might be in a few weeks. At least marriage is out in the open. Living Together is covert; it's underground marriage.

Living Together seemed a fine idea at the time—until everybody started doing it, which took all the wickedness out of it. It went from *avant-garde* to yesterday's mashed potatoes; from there it was but a short hop to national pastime. Today, Living Together is fat and bald. Some couples have been living together longer than their parents were married.

From its original loose make-it-up-as-you-go-along and let's-play-hippie state, Living Together gradually hardened into humdrum unholy wedlock. It lost its funky free-spirited feel, back in the days when you could still shock people. Shocking people now requires at least two illegitimate offspring.

All sorts of quite ordinary, conventional people started Living Together—accountants, real estate agents, firemen, librarians, Republicans. Only the weird and offbeat went through the barbaric ritual of a wedding, with ministers and bridesmaids and honeymoons.

Living Together is a threat to single people, even more than marriage, which you can get a handle on. When someone is married, that's it; they're gone. Marriage is above-board, like singledom, but there's something sneaky about Living Together.

Live Togethers smudge the lines and pollute the social ecology. They're slippery—mermaids and eunuchs. You never know where you are with Live Togethers. If a married person flirts, it's serious business. When a Live Together flirts, it's just to stay in practice.

Live Togethers, besides being teases, are above the battle, aloof from both married and single life. They've made wishy-washiness an alternate lifestyle. Living Together is unfair to unorganized singles. Say you meet someone at a party who is quite fabulous. She has no ring and is wandering around, giving off single vibes. You ask someone about her and are told, "Oh, she's living with someone." You feel doublecrossed.

And just what *are* single vibes? Do they in fact exist or are they a figment of my overactive imagination? Can they be simulated with laboratory rats? Yes.

Live Togethers act unlike married people. They dress cuter. They still look around a little, just in case. They laugh louder. They leave parties later. They mingle more. They are not attached at the elbow. They exude singleosity. All of which is highly deceptive and cruel to singles, who have a rough enough time threading their way through mobs of married couples.

Indeed, many people who live together even stoop to having babies, which is about as low as you can get.

I think it only fair that Live Togethers display some sort of warning badge, like a wedding cake with a red line through it. Actually, Live Togethers should go to parties only with their own kind; that'll teach 'em.

Modern couples fighting the yuppie influence are searching for a more *au courant* way of being uncommitted. Living Together served that purpose handily for years but is now, in the eyes of many (and the law), neo-marriage.

Since Living Together has legal status and little sex appeal, there's a real need for a new alternate lifestyle, something to put the sin back into living in sin. A classic *ménage à trois* is one possible way to go.

There are some drawbacks to it (more shoes scattered about than usual, less time in the bathroom, etc.), but the advantages are endless, chief among them being one additional person to make the bed. Then, too, if you have an argument and somebody moves out, there's still a chance to make a go of it.

IN DEFENSE OF SINGLES BARS

YOU DON'T WANT to hear this, but there is something to be said for singles bars. Not a whole lot, granted, but something, and here it is: they're the fastest, most efficient mating dance yet devised. I didn't say easy, fun, civilized or honorable.

A singles bar is social hardball, the brutal facts: *Here I am everybody. Love me or leave me.* It's your basic no-nonsense screen test. Even if they don't work, they offer hope to those who might otherwise wander the streets alone, desperate dateaholics.

The personals ad is a more discreet forum, but no matter how you cut it, an ad is an ad: all promises and claims, artfully composed, but only two-dimensional. What a classified ad lacks, no matter how carefully and cleverly worded, is *vibes*—eye contact, flesh and blood, sinew and bone. Chemistry. A singles bar is a bubbling cauldron of sexual alchemy, a body language lab. Precisely how one leans, looks, talks, the way one cradles a glass or laughs is worth $500 in opera tickets, wine tastings and quiet walks in the country.

Many a paper tiger is a weasel in the not-too-solid flesh. A singles saloon, once you can push yourself there, is no worse than most parties with a no-host bar. Pretend it's a party you've crashed. As at most cocktail parties, everyone's waiting for something transcendent to happen that rarely does. Ah, but it may, it may.

Here, at least, nobody knows you. If you creep away or stand glumly alone, it's your secret. If nothing else, a singles bar provides elbow room. It also lets you begin all over again each time. Reinvent yourself. Make your own personality sundae.

A personals ad is a polite blind date. A fern bar is the law of the jungle: crude, often humiliating, even dehumanizing, but there's no flowery verbiage to hide behind, no dreamy imagery. Best of all, you don't pay by the word, and there's no registration fee.

True, it lacks social grace. To stroll into a singles bar, or any singles dance, and say, "Let's have a real warm welcome for Me!," requires the grit and spirit of Scarlett O'Hara.

It takes a stout heart to attend any officially sanctioned "singles" event. Just to walk in and find a corner is a harrowing challenge. Waiting to be singled out requires nerves of steel. Not everyone's up to it. Actually, nobody's up to it, but some brave souls do it anyway—put themselves on the line and, almost always, vow never to go back.

Most people can't do it and won't do it; they prefer luck. Singles bars habitues are just trying to give luck a little nudge.

Psyching up oneself helps. What you must do, simply, is tell yourself (or whoever you meet) that you're writing a paper on social interaction; a play, a poem, a column. This quickly (1) removes you from the common herd and (2) makes you seem terribly interesting.

Jane Austen claimed that "everything happens at parties." If Jane were hanging out now, I suspect she'd be sitting in a corner booth at Margaritaville, noting the intricate social mesh in needlepoint prose.

Possibly nothing happens at singles bars. Could be they don't work and have outlived their original purpose. Clubs and classes may have rendered them as useless a dating antique as the box social and the minuet, but relationship lectures take time, money and ego, and they put you to sleep.

If a pottery class or a love seminar turns up a roomful of zeros, you've lost $75 and six evenings, whereas a singles bar gets to the point, that point being: Is there anyone among these 73 footloose folks who makes my heart leap up and do a little jig?

You saunter in, you scan the room, you leave or you hang around 40 minutes and then leave, casting no shadow. You may erase the entire thing from memory.

The only people I ever meet in singles bars are people I already know, or once took out. One grins sheepishly, exchanges pleasantries, perhaps meets the new beau and slips out into the calm, anonymous night.

Singles bars are worse in the abstract than in fact. Most people in singles bars are, yes, actual human beings, largely solid law-abiding citizens, with jobs and homes and parents and dogs and IRAs and leaky roofs and everything.

Best of all, there's an instant built-in rapport among singles bar folks. After 45 minutes, you both agree you can't stand the place and whatever follows is sure to seem delightful by comparison.

Indeed, the worse the singles bar, the better time you'll have chuckling about it later—a firm basis for a relationship.

LITTLE GRAY LIES

A S ONE OF SIX males on a "Panel of Bachelors," a veritable cross-section of mankind, I faced a roomful of curious females hoping to learn What Men Want. During the evening's cross-examination, I was struck by several things—and not one of them, to my delight, a custard pie.

The first is that women—at least the thirty women gathered anxiously in the Barcelona II Room of the Ramada Renaissance Hotel—are still confused by the male animal, even though they claim to read us like a book, and a fairly well-thumbed one at that.

A second revelation is that men don't know why women are so confused. Just be yourself, we insisted, after which one woman rose to read a list of twenty-five things we had previously said women should be, all conflicting.

Someone said that being told to be herself is no help at all. They are themselves, presumably, but it never seems enough somehow. The women I've known are mostly themselves with men. Men are mostly themselves without women. I have no idea how to resolve this.

As an example of the confusion, misunderstanding and doubletalk that goes on, take the question one woman asked: "Why do men say they'll call and don't?"

Are men born liars, as she hints? No, I think we mean it when we say it, but even if we don't it's nothing more devious than a social cliche, like "See you later," which we tell people whom we have absolutely no plan to see later.

Nonetheless, women claim that such phrases should not be flung about carelessly because they're taken seriously. I say it's only a lie if you look somebody soulfully in the eyes and say, "I'll call you," and don't. Anyway, women say stuff like "I had fun" and "Call me sometime" when they mean quite the opposite.

When men don't call, *why* don't they? It's not always mere

thoughtlessness or amnesia. Men change their minds (a little-known male prerogative); they lose heart; they don't get around to it for six weeks and are too embarrassed; they meet other women and get sidetracked; they can't remember why they called in the first place.

When men don't call on purpose, why don't they? Not calling seems a torturous rejection, but it's really just a way of bowing out gracefully, eloquently and maybe cowardly. It's a way of saying good-by without rubbing it in. Not calling is the male no thank you; the female version is not returning phone calls.

It seems rude, but is there an alternative? "Hi, I'm just calling to say I won't be calling you anymore—i.e., we shall not be going out again."

Or is there some sort of classic Bogart approach? "Hello, kid. It's me. Why haven't I called? Simple, sweetheart. It's all over, through, finished. You and I never did have a future. Sorry, toots, but life plays funny tricks when you're single. See ya around." It sounds great in the fog after a troubled affair in Casablanca, but I doubt if it would go over at the Blue Lite Café.

You could always try this: "Hello, Amy? Sorry I haven't called but, well, it was just one of those things, just one of those crazy flings, one of those bells that now and then rings, just one of those things. If we'd thought a bit 'bout the end of it when we started painting the town, we'd have been aware that this love affair was too hot not to cool down. So good-by, farewell and amen . . . "

Once, as a kind of experiment, I wrote a note to someone I'd been dating casually (drowsily, in fact) and explained why I wouldn't be calling—someone had come along and I was un-single, effective immediately.

It wasn't a true Dear John letter, but she said it wasn't necessary to explain. She seemed too understanding, I thought. It was a gentlemanly gesture yet a mite presumptuous; it assumed she'd be crestfallen not to hear from me.

Once, somebody I'd seen five times called to ask why I hadn't called in many months. I felt like a rat, trapped and traumatized. After apologetic mumbles and assurances that it was nothing personal, I said I'd been seeing one person, which was only half untrue.

The true unspoken half is that we'd dated ourselves into a box—a common occurrence—and reached a crucial point where the only way out was onward and upward. If there's no upward mobility, it seems a bigger lie to go out just to be nice. Mercy dating.

I operate on the general, if shaky, assumption that if I've lost interest, so has she. At one point, I asked our rapt crowd at the Panel of Bachelors if women ever go out when they don't want to. All said no. I also operate on the equally shaky rule: *If in doubt, don't go out.*

UNCIVIL WAR BETWEEN TWO STATES

I HAVE DEVISED A NEW WORD for my confirmed un-single friends, whom I term "marriageists"—or, in extreme cases, "monophobes."

A marriageist is a professional, long-term and, sad to say, somewhat smug married person who makes fun of those in the wild, perplexed, untamed state of singlehood.

Marriageists tend to be superior about their coupled state—especially nowadays, when married life is the safest sex around—and they look down on the unmarried person as a shameless, sorry ne'er-do-well.

Marriageists wonder when singles will quit frittering around and get a real job. They think we singles are not serious about life, that we are selfish, wishy-washy, spoiled, picky, various vile things. They don't quite say it but we can feel it; one senses monophobia in the air.

Single people do not go around denigrating marital bliss, not publicly. Oh, we may have our doubts, or snicker in the privacy of our homes, but we don't go about bad-mouthing barbecues and sneering at wedding albums.

Recently, one marriageist friend said, "Don't you find dating exhausting?" Another sighed, "Dating is *such* a game." A third monophobe scoffed, "I don't know anyone who still uses the word 'date,'" as if it was not only a lower life form—sort of a sponge with a foldup toothbrush—but also a prehistoric one; she made the word "date" sound faintly dirty, and foolish.

All of which, naturally, threw me on the defensive, a common position for us 2,038 remaining singles. Let us examine these wild charges:

"Dating is exhausting": Agreed, but so is marriage, losing weight, touring Europe, whipping up a pot roast or any worthwhile pursuit. The implication, of course, is that it's not only exhausting but pointless, which of course misses the point of d——g.

Most people don't date just to date, unless they're into masochism. The idea, as I understand it, is that each first date could, with luck, be your last first date. The more dates, the better your odds of quitting.

"Dating is such a game": It is indeed but much more interesting than basketball or poker, which it often resembles, or "Jeopardy," with which it also shares something in common.

Domesticity is another form of game, only the rules are rather more complex. Games are fun if the players are skilled and know a few clever moves you haven't seen before.

The game aspect is precisely what makes dating a popular if maligned pastime and why, I suspect, marriageists secretly envy it. What, after all, is marriage but a doubles game played with one racket?

To flog this metaphor one last paragraph, marriageists are also reminiscent of retired ball-players who, watching from the sidelines, would love to get to play a few innings, even in an oldtimers' game.

"Nobody 'dates' anymore": Despite its current slump, it remains a common practice among certain unenlightened urban peoples who, through education, may someday pull themselves up to a more civilized domestic level.

Around the office, the marriageists often gang up and toss wisecracks at the accursed single. If you show someone around the office, and it happens to be a female someone, the joshing does not die down for days. Two married women can concoct the smarmiest interrogations of all, giggling and batting their eyes should you carelessly mention a female twice. "Oh-h-h, *really?!*" they titter. Married men are worse; they want the graphic details.

By the same token, married people expect singles to listen to amusing tales of domestic life (Kids Say the Darnedest Things Department). We listen politely, nodding and grinning at the appropriate lines. If I had any nerve, I'd buttonhole a couple of these proud parents and make them listen to all the bright little remarks that my date made the night before.

WELCOME TO THE SINGLE ZONE

NOT LONG AGO ON TV, they tried to revive "The Twilight Zone," but none of the shows included the weird and unusual episodes that occur with alarming regularity in . . . *The Single Zone*:

You are on a date. You have never been to a movie with this woman before. The two of you enter the theater and glance at each other to see who will decide where to sit. She begins to walk toward the front, you hang back. She munches popcorn; you hate the smell of popcorn in movies. The two of you have just entered . . . *The Single Zone*.

There are hundreds of such twilight areas that one must neatly negotiate. We will attempt to visit a few. First, that vast uncharted space between the couch and the bedroom, where anything can happen and invariably does:

You are on the sofa, necking. The mirrors have begun to steam up. Clothing is falling this way and that. Torsos are becoming grotesquely intertwined. Wine glasses are crashing to the floor. The record is stuck. She says, "I suppose I should flip it over . . . "

Another one way trip into *The Single Zone*:

You've been seeing a woman six months and things are going nicely. When you begin to stay over, she gracefully provides a toothbrush, green in color. One night, preparing for bed, you observe that the green toothbrush is gone; in its place, a shiny new yellow one. Deedeedeedeedeedeedee. . . .

For your further consideration:

You have just left a restaurant. It's your second date, but it's only 9:30, too early to call it an evening and yet too late for a movie. You turn on the ignition. You look at the person in the next seat. She stares ahead. You start the car and begin driving, aimlessly. Your date asks, "Where are we going?"

Or join us now for this other-worldly incident:

Mr. Henry Gardner has been out a few times with Arlene Webber but has decided that it's not going anywhere. He decides to let it slide. One day, Mr. Gardner is at his desk contemplating that evening's date with someone new when the phone rings and an eerie voice says, "Hi. It's Arlene. I wondered if there was some reason you hadn't called?"

Another journey into the realm of the half-understood:

You are at a party given by a new man at the office. Over cocktails, you observe a fabulous looking woman. You noticeably eyeball her. She gazes at you in a friendly but funny way, which you interpret as a come-hither glance. You walk over, excitedly, and chat her up furiously, during which exchange you realize she's the host's wife.

Here is yet one more classic bizarre tale from the beyond:

You've been going out with someone for six months and both of you are looking forward to New Year's Eve, though nothing specifically has been said about it. A week before Christmas, you fall madly in love with someone else. That very week, your regular date calls and says, "Put on your dancin' shoes, kid, we got invited to a great New Year's Eve party!"

Or what of this odd visitor from Out There?:

You are in bed with Miss Pretty Good. The phone rings. She says, "You better answer that." You say, "Nah, it's probably just a drunk." She says, "Maybe it's an emergency." You fall out of bed and stumble nakedly into the hall to pick up the phone. It's an old girlfriend calling from New York, where it's midnight. "Guess who?" she says. You guess who and she adds, "How *are* you, anyway! Hey, can you talk?" From the bedroom, a small voice calls out, "Sweetie, who is it?"

This ride into *The Single Zone* defies explanation:

Your best friend has been going with someone you think is a perfect match, except he's too dumb to realize it and you can see she's rapidly losing interest. You have lunch with her, hoping to talk her into not giving up just yet, but before you can bring up their relationship you feel a stocking foot rubbing against your leg.

Finally, from a distant corner of *The Single Zone*, this:

You're out with someone you find extremely attractive but remote, dining at the Mesquite Café Bar & Grill. It's the third date—make or break, tonight or never. You ask her how she's been? "Better," she says, "but I was sick as a dog for two weeks."

"That's too bad," you say. "You're OK now, I hope."

"Oh, yeah, fine. Quite a scare, though. I thought I was pregnant."

LIFESTYLES OF THE FAMOUS AND LONELY

FROM THE PEOPLE'S ALMANAC, I have in my hand a list of "Noted People Who Never Married," which is interesting but unhelpful. What the People's Almanac fails to do is tell why these great catches never married, which I will now explain for the next edition.

Jane Addams, social settlement worker: Addams was a real downer. "Lighten up, Jane!" guys told her, but she wore her heart on her sleeve. All she ever talked about on dates was the poor and homeless. A nice woman, with a darling smile and a wide variety of bonnets, just not a whole lot of laughs. Jane would ask excited men back to "my house" only to give them a tour of Hull House, her shelter.

Ludwig von Beethoven, composer: Something of a grouch, but, when you got to know him, a wicked cut-up. His deafness caused

a few misunderstandings with women, many of whom found him a workaholic.

Jane Austen, English novelist: A little bookish for some guys, but, when Jane took off her glasses, an incredible flirt. In her 50s, she liked picking up young guys.

James Buchanan, 15th president: Was tongue-tied and a terrible dancer. Some said he may have been gay, but women who knew him said no, Jim was just a wimp.

Frederic Chopin, composer and pianist: An inveterate womanizer and all wrapped up in himself. Said one disappointed lover, "Fred never called."

Emily Dickinson, poet: A real sad sack. In the words of an old boyfriend, "Em refused to go anywhere. I'd ask her to a show and she'd say that some dopey flower in her garden was enough show for her. This kind of thing can really turn a guy off."

Elizabeth I, queen of England: Always too busy to make time for the men in her life, none of whom felt they could compete with her. "I don't mind a gal making more money than I do," wrote the Earl of Essex, "but I couldn't stand Liz's patronizing attitude."

J. Edgar Hoover, director of FBI: Could be overly protective; liked to frisk on the first date. One longtime female friend said, "I just never felt Eddie trusted me. You can't build a relationship on distrust."

Susan B. Anthony, women's rights leader: No sense of humor was Sue's major problem. Smart as a whip, yes; a good personality, sure; attractive, in a plain Early American sort of way. But she couldn't take a joke; unsightly dandruff didn't help either.

Henry James, novelist: "Your basic Mr. Snob, y'know what I'm saying?" recalled one ex-date. "I mean, we're talking top hats, wing collars, swallowtails, the whole bit. At first, it was fun but then it became a drag. I always thought he was bisexual but Henry insisted he was foppish. I finally had it with that entire fop scene."

Joan of Arc, saint: Her odd lifestyle kept away men, who considered her trouble. "I like a woman with some fire, but Joanie is too weird," one steady beau noted. "We'd be having a nice dinner and she'd start talking to voices. It ruined our sex life, too. I can take a Jewish princess, but a Catholic saint is too heavy. I broke it off."

Sir Isaac Newton, physicist: A nervous guy, especially around fruit. After the apple incident, he was never really the same, living in fear that something, or some woman, might fall on him. "The man definitely knew his forces of gravity but that's it," said a female friend. "I told him, 'Ike, life is more than "what goes up must come down."'"

Florence Nightingale, hospital reformer: Liked to feel wanted yet couldn't relate to one person's needs. "She has to comfort all goddamn humanity," said a man who dated her right after the Crimean War. "Flo could be a real bitch if you didn't succor the needy her way."

Alexander Pope, satiric poet: A bit of a wise ass. Women found him sexy, despite his hump, but rather cold. "He'd like write me these huge epic poems, but then I wouldn't hear from him for months," a former lover complained. "Al Pope was a great cook, too, which a lot of people forget. His chili was to die over!"

Arthur Schopenhauer, philosopher: Had trouble with intimacy. One woman said, "I always thought he was a mama's boy. Too bad. Artie could be a real sweet guy."

Adam Smith, economist: A terrible skinflint and, according to one ex-lover, also smelled funny.

Henry David Thoreau, author: A loner but, to his pal Emerson, "a *mensch*." One diary entry by a former lover says: "Dave was attentive—he'd give you the shirt off his back—but he was just so into himself. He had a lot going for him, however the guy was totally repressed."

Toulouse-Lautrec, painter: Worried about his physical appearance but liked hookers, who found him a terrific talker and, despite his height, a good listener.

THE OLD PAL NETWORK

I 'M LOSING A friend in a few months. He's not dying or moving to Europe. Worse. He's getting married.

This is not a generous view, I concede, but then his is a serious breach of faith, a callous breaking of single ties. Some bachelors view married life as the enemy—not for ourselves, necessarily, but always for our friends. Ever since college, I've felt it's rather rude of old buddies to get engaged without first consulting me.

I pretend to be delighted for them, and in a vague way, I am. It's me I'm unhappy about—or rather, *us*. We had a nice thing going; why louse it up?

Married women look upon bachelors as members of the underground. It's well known that certain wives won't allow their husbands to associate with single men, for fear we may be catching, silent carriers of a virulent strain of wildness or, more dangerously, well-being.

They suspect we sit around whispering in the ears of innocent husbands, leading them down the garden path, like the fox luring Pinocchio—whose song, "I've Got No Strings on Me," is the bachelors' national anthem.

Less discussed, though, is the feeling among single men of being sold down the river when a friend decides to throw him over (not him, *them*—buddyhood) for a mere wonderful woman.

Most couples maintain unwed friends as surrogate singles, sort of faithful retainers they keep around to hear how the other half lives. They're Upstairs, with the *au pairs* and baby buggies, while we, Downstairs, are called upon to report in with amusing and scandalous tales of life among the squalid dating class.

When an old friend, even a woman, marries, I take it personally, as a subtle rebuke to a way of life we not only once shared but secretly, silently championed.

I admit to feeling dark treasonous pangs whenever a close friend crosses over to the married side, never to be heard from again, at least not in quite the same way.

A good friend who marries is still around, halfway, but without the private jokes, conspiratorial winks and last-minute pizza dinners. Now when I visit, we must meet in committee. All plans need to be cleared, seconded and written in triplicate.

A man I know who lives with someone complains he feels guilty if he sees me, or any man, more than twice a week. Once is OK, twice is borderline OK, three times and he detects a definite cooling trend at home. When we go to a movie, I feel like his mistress.

Recently, one old friend got married, and now another is mulling it over. I'm not into male bonding (or any other form of S&M), but one of the simpler, non-swinging joys of single life is its bachelor camaraderie.

To a bachelor, anyone's marriage threatens to break up the act. It's more fun being single with someone who's also flying solo. This is the old clubhouse mentality, where girls are appreciated and tolerated but not allowed in because they get in the way of more important things, like baseball, Jewish princess jokes and general boorishness.

Every so often, I meet for lunch with two recently remarried friends—one man, one woman—who always ask who I'm seeing, have stopped seeing, is not seeing me, etc. Innermost secrets are divulged.

With the woman, it's the same, but with the man it's different than when he was one of us, a member in good standing of The Boys. Oh, he's interested, but when he asks what's happening, it's almost as if he's inquiring about my folks. Indeed, his advice now takes on a faintly parental tone.

I politely inquire into his married life, but my heart's not in it, and he knows it. Marriage isn't as sexy, at least not to outsiders, or maybe just too complex to get into. Babies are beyond my comprehension. He soaks up all the lurid details of singlehood while I smile weakly at junior's latest rejoinder.

It gives men a feeling of strength (warmth, anyway) to meet regularly and swap the talk of buccaneer bachelors. I don't mean a night out with the guys: no bowling, poker or saloons. Guys in groups terrify me. I just mean the jolly one-on-one banter and *bonhomie* of my loyal unmarried brothers.

Among single men, one's company, two's a crowd.

THE BACHELOR'S GUIDE TO BABIES

ALL OF MY LIFE, I have been beset by babies. They attack me on purpose, knowing that I am vulnerable, unable to function around small children, let alone infants.

Most kids patronize me, the younger ones especially. They're snooty, uncommunicative and suspicious of my shy, well-meaning advances. Toddlers take a special delight in provoking me. More than anything else, they love to watch single men squirm.

I take their assaults personally. I used to think it was mere coincidence that kids kept turning up wherever I was, but now I realize there's an underground moppet mafia whose primary function is to turn me into a sputtering wreck.

Why else would children pop up in intimate restaurants where

I'm dining? They don't like Cajun food, I'm fairly sure. Babies just seem to have it in for me. What do they want?

Recently, flying back from New York, I was on a jumbo jet with 300 seats, on which I counted five kids, ages six months to 4 years—each and every tot seated within earshot. They were subdued until the smallest one noticed me and let out a howl of delight (the international baby signal) that set off his four accomplices. For the next six hours, my non-smoking section became a flying day-care center.

A week ago, I was seated in a bagelry at 7:30 A.M., minding my business, when the place began filling up with nefarious wee folk, just as cranky as could be and spoiling for a fight. One little girl scanned the room, saw me and realized she'd found a sitting duck.

Don't tell me these are random occurrences that "could happen to anyone." The fact is, they don't happen to anyone; I've checked. Parents think I'm paranoid, though. For years, I thought I might be, but now I've got proof that children *do* follow me around.

They've been dispatched to wipe me out or win me over, trying to lower my built-in resistance to people under the age of nine. They used to be subtler about it, but they're singling me out, dispatching kids in vast numbers. There's no place I can go where a baby won't arrive in moments, as if by accident.

"Why not notify the police?" you ask. I used to call the cops, but they looked the other way, saying that bachelor abuse is beyond their jurisdiction. I need witnesses and physical evidence, almost impossible to come up with. Tots are into psychological terrorism.

Bachelors and babies are natural enemies, with a long-simmering history of dark suspicion. Women always want to know if you like kids. If you say yes, the pink flows back into their cheeks. When asked the inevitable baby question, I flinch. The query comes in two parts: Part I: "Do you have any kids?" And if not, why not, or Part II: "Do you want any?" My answers tend to be "No" and "Not quite," but I may fudge Part II ("Just not sure . . . Depends. I've *thought* about it. This is great mousse.").

Babies are impossible to deal with on a one-to-one basis. I never know where I stand with them. They're ruthless. Some babies pretend to find me irresistible—until I fall for it and try to make friends, whereupon they want no more to do with me. They were just teasing, testing my will, waiting for me to crack.

Once in a while, I meet someone with pre-teen kids, who at least know the language even if they don't always speak it. You can make a joke, you can pander, but there's no getting through to a baby—not and still maintain some measure of dignity.

A sure way to strike out with a five-year-old is to lower yourself to his level. Why is this even necessary? It seems that once in a while a kid could at least attempt to make *me* feel at ease, yet they refuse to extend themselves even a little; most infants won't even meet you half-way. They don't need to, and they know it.

Babies have it too soft. They think it's enough to roll around and babble. A grownup is expected to coo in return and make a clown of himself. If the baby grins, an adult is delirious with joy; grownups are too easily amused by babies.

Me, I won't play their silly little games. I doubt if babies respect adults who make teeny voices and screw up their noses and behave in a goofy manner. Deep down, the baby is disgusted. No wonder, years later, a teenager won't take adults seriously. By the age of six, he's already thinking, *Why should I listen to this schmuck?*

The trouble with babies is, they're too young, also undersized. While this is often cited as a large part of their charm, it hinders the flow of conversation. Put me in a room with a kid, and I am quickly humiliated, defensive and speechless. They look to me like alien creatures.

Contrary to all their hype, babies by and large are not cute. OK, some of them are—maybe 20 percent, at most—but they're not that cute. Come on, folks, let's get a grip on ourselves. Nothing is *that* adorable, except maybe me in my little sailor suit at the age of four. If you want to see cute, I'll show you cute.

I'VE GOT A CRUSH ON YOU, YOU AND YOU

NOT ENOUGH HAS been said about the crush as an art form, a poem of heartfelt inexpression. There are degrees of crushiness, from the totally dopey and boyish to the fervent and semi-crazed, to what a friend calls disguised lust.

Like most singles, I am an expert on crushes, which I have tried to swear off as a juvenile habit, a sort of acne of the heart. It is a form of addiction, often fatal but, one hopes, some day curable. Most marriages, after all, begin as crushes, though most don't move beyond the idiot state of a mild romantic rush.

February 14 celebrates romantic idiocy. If St. Patrick's Day is amateur night for drunks, St. Valentine's Day is for amateur lovers. It is the day to commemorate passionate affairs, passing fancies, fatal attractions, lunatic fantasies, mushy romances and, most of all, tender crushes.

In my past, I have developed crushes every few days, or gone for months totally de-crushed, burnt out. I get crushes on women glimpsed in bus windows, on voices, on Macy's models, on actresses in milk commercials. I get crushes on women in 1910 photographs, on old flames who flicker in memory, on waitresses, meter maids, women on talk shows and magician's assistants.

The list is endless and mindless. I've had crushes on Harriet Nelson, dancers in chorus lines, Jean Kennedy Smith, John Singer Sargent portraits, 800 operators. I don't get star crushes often, but a few include Myrna Loy, Dorothy McGuire, Diana Quick, Elizabeth McGovern and Debra Winger. My earliest crush was Margaret O'Brien. Were any of the above to arrive on my doorstep, I would ooze into a pool of melted butter.

My crush career began at an early age, with Fritzi Ritz, Lois Lane and the voice of Margo Lane on "The Shadow." This evolved into snipping out the heads of selected girls in fifth-grade class pictures, leaving the photo riddled with ovals. I still know all their names but would not reveal them even to the FBI.

My first severe crush was on a fourth-grade teacher, the beauteous, fragile and creamy Miss Julian. I didn't even know what a crush was but I had one on Miss Julian that surpassed Cyrano's for Roxanne.

I refused to admit it, sure it was evidence of some perverse quirk, this vague longing for a grown woman, perhaps as old as 28—a love that dare not speak its name. I graduated to major crushes in high school that burned for years, resulting in an affliction of the larynx prevalent in 15-year-old boys who, upon dialing their heart's desire and hearing her voice, turn to pillars of salt.

For five years, I carried a crush—a sort of unlit torch—for a Miss Gail Wilson, whose very name, decades after, stirs old embers. Years later, I saw her, pregnant, standing in line at the Department of Motor Vehicles, and again was dumbstruck, also mildly shocked at her condition.

In school, I had half a dozen major crushes that I took so seriously I'd rank them by intensity, juggling their names in my head, or on the flap of my plain brown book jacket. I rarely, if ever, spoke to them, which is the best way to nourish a nice, fat rosy crush.

Once you make yourself known, and actually engage the crushee in live conversation, it leaves the realm of crushdom and enters real life, where all hell breaks loose. The worst thing for a crush is to confront it openly. To keep a crush burning, stoke it secretly.

This is where St. Valentine's Day comes in. The valentine is the subtlest romantic medium ever devised. It allows crushers, without saying so openly, to tell the crushees of their feelings, however wild and impossible—the more wildly impossible, the better. The valentine is a mute proposal from the heart. Crushees say it without flowers; they say it with silence.

In a way, it's the perfect mode of expression in the Age of Noncommitment. I once left a valentine on someone's doorstep, unsigned. If you have to sign the thing, forget it; an outright declaration ruins it. The object of my devotion said nothing when we met again, which told me she had received my heartfelt message.

IS IT A BIRD? A PLANE?
NO . . . IT'S *SINGLEMAN!*

WHILE READING OF plans to modernize Superman's image, I became aware that all of our great fictional heroes are single. Fairly startling and oddly encouraging. Try these role models on for size:

The Lone Ranger, Sherlock Holmes, Batman, The Shadow, Don Quixote, Wonder Woman, Mickey Mouse, Prince Valiant, Plastic Man, Robin Hood, Roy Rogers, Popeye, Jack Armstrong, Joe Palooka, Sam Spade, Nero Wolfe—each and every one, single as single can be.

Why do married people get no respect in pop fiction? Nick and Nora Charles and Rhett and Scarlett are the only heroic pairs who come to mind. Is it that their creators were all single? No, I think the answer, painful as it may be, is that there is something inherently heroic about one person battling the forces of evil. *Two* people battling the forces of evil in tandem is dull. My question is, why?

Most all of these heroes had sidekicks—sometimes women (Olive Oyl, Effie, Dale Evans) but usually men. Hmm. As has long been rumored, Batman and Robin, Holmes and Watson and the Lone Ranger and Tonto are closet gays.

Maybe all our fictional heroes are single so that nobody can come between, say, Superman and us devoted readers. If Superman and Lois were a pair, females couldn't fantasize about the Clark Kent in their lives, and men couldn't fantasize about Superman. Or Lois.

The Lone Ranger had classic single-guy traits (rarely home, career-centered, ate out a lot), except that he revealed not a flicker of interest in women. Even Roy, Gene and Hopalong Cassidy acknowledged women's presence. The Lone Ranger was oblivious to females, unless they were helpless widows with crackly voices.

Was the Lone Ranger a misogynist? Did he prefer Indian girls? Mourning a lost love from his Texas Ranger days?

Though Sherlock Holmes had a crush on Irene Adler, he seemed to regard women as an inferior, often lethal, species. Holmes was a classic bachelor, Henry Higgins with a spy glass, too self-involved for a mate.

I suspect all these people are single because, if a hero or heroine is involved romantically, he or she might lose their passionate concern for justice or adventure. Readers would feel Holmes' powers were eroded by shopping for lamb chops and fixing screen doors.

To be sure, Superman and the Lone Ranger kept strange hours. They were always away weekends, pursuing evildoers; they didn't do lunch or know about quality time. Yet in a way these guys were ideal mates—loyal, dedicated, with high moral characters, forever being tested. I can't imagine the Lone Ranger chasing dance-hall girls or Superman playing poker until all hours.

Any idea of making Superman a modern single guy will lead to his undoing, subtly altering his ambiguous, confused relationship with Ms. Lane.

Now that Clark Kent has become a television newscaster in the recently revised version, it's sure to change things with Lois, who (after covering women's issues) feels she doesn't need a man. He'll go fat sitting around reporting on mass transit ("Since when is the mayor more powerful than a locomotive?") and high-rises ("cost overruns leap tall buildings in a single bound").

All of this is likely to shake up Superman and give him a mid-life crisis. He'll have to seek counseling to learn why he can't sustain a relationship with anyone other than Lois Lane and why, with her, he can't even consummate it.

When she's not wondering why Kent is such a wimp, she's pining for Superman, with whom she has the longest unresolved relationship in singles history. She won't look at anyone else, and he won't look at her, lowering her self-esteem and making her more dependent on him than she'll admit. Besides which, Lois is near the end of her child-bearing years and perhaps has begun to consider Clark as Mr. Possible.

In his new guise, Kent might seem more appealing to her now that he's not just another general-assignment reporter who hadn't written a story in 45 years, though it could make him more attractive to other women on the staff and convince him to dump Lois.

Imagine Superman suddenly thrust into the middle of the Me Generation. He becomes less socially concerned and finds he can't knock out apartheid with a mighty *sock!!* He'll find himself bored by fighting crime, more interested in protecting property than lives. When he vanishes, he ducks into his men's club, removes his clothes, takes a sauna, sips a martini and reads Forbes. As a new single, Superman may delay fighting crime if it means skipping a new Thai restaurant.

The Man of Steel, although into keeping fit, begins pampering himself, afraid to injure his body punching out thugs. As a modern guy, he's sure to become *too* vulnerable to cry, sympathizing with the plight of the criminal underclass. He'll be less prone to violence, preferring to sit down with Luther and have him express his hostilities about his sociopathic feelings.

Worst of all, a modernized Superman will be little help to people in trouble who summon his aid: *"I am not available now. At the beep, please give your name and dilemma. I will return your call for help as soon as possible."*

ADVICE TO THE MARRIAGE-LORN

I N THE 1940S and '50s, there was a radio soap opera called "The Romance of Helen Trent," a daily trauma that asked the question, "Can a woman over 35 find romance?"

Like today's woman over 35, Helen found romance aplenty (in daily 15-minute doses, all of it troubled), yet never a man she could call home. But did Helen whimper? Did she mutter, "There's noth-

ing but jerks and weirdos out there?" Did she bemoan the lack of
men willing to make a commitment? Did she insist that all the
best guys were either gay or taken? She did not.

Helen Trent was single before there were stats claiming her
chances of marrying after 35 were a scary five percent and dwin-
dling hourly—which flies in the face of last season's surveys,
which insisted that marriage was the hottest thing since duck
pâté.

Still, today's Helen Trent is convinced she's doomed to sit out
her days alone, waiting for a phone to ring or a ring to appear. Ms.
Trent, your modern unmarried career woman (you remember
her—the one who wanted it all), feels oppressed, cut down in her
prime by a plague of wimps and playboys, bachelor frogs raining
down on her and no sign of a prince riding to the rescue in a white
Porsche.

As a man well past 35 and searching (OK, browsing), I feel like
the partial cause of all this despair, but what have we done, me and
my crummy ilk? Plenty, claim women, unfurling a roster of bad
attitudes:

Men Don't Want to Get Married. Not to anybody of any age,
they claim, no matter how pert and unlined, because it's more fun
to play the field. Well, the field ain't that great—crowded, yes, but
so is the freeway at rush hour.

Even for a gnarled single guy like me, domesticity remains the
ultimate fantasy. Marriage is what romance used to be, some
shimmering Shangri-La where sex once gamboled. Sex had to cut
back on its gamboling and has become as routine as repainting the
kitchen.

Anyone can find a cozy rose-covered romance just by scanning
the classifieds (the question is, can you lock it in at a 30-year fixed
rate?), so marriage is the new romantic ideal, and the longer you're
single the more golden it seems.

Marriage is also less hazardous to your health, and cheaper.
Merely as a shrewd business deal, it makes sense—and keeps you
out of studio apartments and doctor's offices.

Some women believe that "men don't want to get married"
simply because they don't want to marry *them*.

There Are Lots of Interesting Women Out There—all holding empty, wilted dance cards, while cringing against the far wall are mobs of creeps.

Not quite. Interesting and smart is harder to find than pretty or even nice. Nice is nice, but it won't get you through long weekends. You think herpes is bad; try ennui.

Smart doesn't mean a degree in philosophy from Oxford (though it couldn't hurt). I'll settle for a supple turn of mind that doesn't get all its data from "People" and "USA Today," someone who beats me to the punch and can argue without viewing it as character assassination.

Alas, the flip side of bright often tends to be neurotic—women desperate about their lives, bodies, babies (or lack of) and relationships. Lighten up, persons.

Funnier would help—not silly, funny. Funny is a subspecies of smart. I don't mean Joan Rivers; Susan St. James, Shelley Long or Suzanne Pleschette is more the idea—a glint in the eye, a wry word, a bemused air.

Funny does not mean "laughs a lot," as they say in the personals, a sure sign of someone who laughs too much, confusing "sense of humor" with giddiness or a tendency to whoop, the No. 1 leading turnoff. Chuckling is best; cacklers and gigglers need not apply.

There are indeed many lovely and talented women older than 35, but they still have to fit your precise dreamboat specs, and also put up with your own oddities. It's not as easy as choosing the best avocado; the avocado has to choose you back.

Also, the older one gets, of either domestic persuasion, the longer one's list of unnegotiable demands. There's something to be said for marrying before you know too much, learn to spot personality glitches and talk yourself out of it.

With age comes wisdom, but most of all comes pickiness, my chief suspect as the real bad guy, not Men. We're all too spoiled out here in the land of the free and the home of 31 flavors, 48 channels and octoplex theaters. Women are now as choosy as men, and about time, but it halves the odds.

It's a Buyer's Market for Men. True, there are more male than female creatures, but all you need is one. The catch is, men think they need marriage less than women (we need it more, if you're into longevity) and have to be dragged kicking and screaming into domestic bliss. We hate leaving the party before everyone else goes home.

All the Best Men Are Married. And they're married to All the Best Women.

Men Can't Cope with Successful Career Women. The specter of Lady Macbeth still strikes terror in some men's hearts, but success is sexy, and the more money the merrier. Work isn't everything, but, like neatness, it counts. It defines a woman, to men anyway. We boys over-identify with our work, but it would be nice to find a woman who loves her job as much as marriage. Women now have careers but too rarely a calling.

Men Fear Intimacy. Not quite right. Intimacy is lovely—it's being exposed that gives men the creeps. We dislike someone rummaging through our psyche. I know what's in there, and believe me, it's no place for a woman.

Men are like primitives facing a camera. If a woman comes too close, she may steal our soul—identity, anyway. (Our soul is usually shot to hell by the time she arrives on the scene for mopping up duties.)

Men fear being taken over. Women claim to know what's best for us, which we resent because they usually do, but men need to be ornery and wrong-headed; it's part of our basic, lovable natures. Even as we fight it off, we want women to civilize us—when we're in the mood.

What's scary is that women are onto us, while they remain aliens to men. We don't like being totally found out, that male need to be secret (even to ourselves), what we call, with quaint Hemingway bravado, Our Own Man.

Men Only Want to Marry Cute Young Things (preferably just out of pinafores).

The shocking truth about younger women is that they're a swell place to visit but you wouldn't want to live there—scenic detours along the bumpy road down the aisle.

No getting around it—younger women *are* younger, also perky, unmarked and Full of Life, but these are not women you bring home to mom, much less to the kids, although you may bring them home.

The standard tootsie charge is a straw woman. Most young

women (younger than 28) are unformed, unfulfilled and un-lots of other stuff. Like middle-aged men, they still have selves to find and things to work out—you don't want to be one of them.

A 25-year-old may be twinklier, but men cannot live by twinkle alone; we learn this, if we learn anything. Better to warm yourself by a low flame.

All right, then, can a woman older than 35 find a husband? Yes, if he's lucky.

Yet disenchantment shadows us all, especially those who have gone around the circuit once or twice. It gnaws at men who not only fear being disillusioned but who worry about disappointing a decent woman—letting down the team.

At least Helen Trent didn't have to cope with marriage surveys. Nobody older than 31 should read one. They can age a woman overnight.

TRUE (AND FALSE) ROMANCES

SHELLY, THE INCURABLE romantic, called me up at 11:30 the other night.

"Well, I'm in love!" he cried. "I just had to talk with someone. I hope you weren't asleep."

"No, I'm up. When I heard your voice at this hour, I was afraid someone had died."

"Someone has," he whimpered. "Me. I'm in heaven. Can I come over? I have to tell you all about Naomi."

"Right now?" I said, knowing it was hopeless. When Shelly's in love, there's no tomorrow. "OK, come on over."

Shelly was there in minutes, breathless as ever. "How could

this have happened so soon?" I asked. "Last week you broke up with Sally and said you didn't plan to date for six months. You were going to be celibate, remember?"

"Well, that was before I went to Woolworth's—before I saw . . . Naomi." He sighed. "You won't believe this woman when you meet her. I've never been so much in love before."

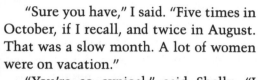

"Sure you have," I said. "Five times in October, if I recall, and twice in August. That was a slow month. A lot of women were on vacation."

"You're so cynical," said Shelly. "I think this is it—the real thing."

"But Shel," I said, "it's *always* the real thing with you. What happened to Gretchen? You know, the manicurist who's getting her Ph.D. in Eastern religions."

"You're getting Gretchen and Greta confused," he said. "But that's old news. Naomi's the only woman for me now. It's incredibly romantic. This could be it—and just when I'd sworn off women, too."

"You swear off women every Monday morning," I said. "You've only known this person 24 hours and you're pledging undying devotion. You'll be married by Friday afternoon."

"Look, it sounds crazy, I admit it. But Naomi's different, believe me."

"It's always different, Shel. Why can't you just take someone out without falling in love with them?"

He said, "I know, but that's my nature. I'm a foolish boy at heart, but the important thing about Naomi is, she's not clingy. She's going to let me have my space. Naomi's a very independent woman, unlike Elaine, who was jealous if I sat next to old ladies on the bus. Naomi told me she needs her space, too. She believes in bunk beds."

"Well, I'm very happy for you," I said. "I hope it lasts at least through Christmas. It's a nice time to have someone special."

"Naomi is *very* special," Shelly smiled seraphically.

"But you said Elaine was very special, and Lois, and Sally, and Martha, and—"

"I was a kid then," protested Shelly. "I've gone through a lot of changes lately. Now I know what I want. Naomi and I have something magical. We want the same things in life."

"But Shel, you've only known her a day."

"Plus a night, don't forget—and *what* a night! How long do you have to know someone to fall in love? We like all the same things—fried calamari, handball, Hitchcock movies, Wynton Marsalis. It seems perfect. What can possibly go wrong?"

"So when do I meet this month's love of your life?"

"I'll bring her by your place after I drop my dinner date off tomorrow night. Will you be home around ten?"

"You mean you're seeing someone else besides Naomi?"

"Yes and no. Look, you can't burn *all* your bridges behind you. Naomi's terrific, but I can't give up Sandy yet. There's something still there, y'know? I love Naomi with every fiber of my being, but I'm still inexplicably tied to Sandy."

"So who's Sandy? You never mentioned a Sandy. Did I ever meet her?"

"Well, no, not yet. She was in your lobby tonight when I came in . . . "

MOVIES ARE CHANCIER THAN EVER

RECENTLY I WENT to see *Crossing Delancey* and found myself in line behind Lenny Waffler, my favorite uncommitted bachelor.

"What are you doing here?" I asked Len. "And why alone?"

"I'm checking out the movie before I take anyone," he said. "I've been doing that a lot, ever since *Kramer vs. Kramer*, which ruined an otherwise terrific potential relationship."

"How so?" I asked, huddling to keep warm.

"Well, the woman I was with had left her husband, just like Meryl Streep did Dustin Hoffman, and she couldn't stand watching it. I had to take her right home afterwards. She didn't say a word the whole way."

"I didn't realize a mere movie could have that effect on your dates?"

"Are you kidding? That's a mild example. I rented *Out of Africa* last week and was humiliated in my own home. It's about this guy who can't commit himself and a woman who wants to possess him. Just what I need. It put a swell damper on the evening."

I said, "I only take women to movies I've seen before. I go to *Singin' in the Rain* a lot."

He explained, "Revivals are perfect for first dates, because you can be pretty sure that any movie made in 1936 won't show two people thrashing around in bed."

Lenny said he's been going to a lot of Sylvester Stallone movies. "They're terrible, sure, but there's nothing in *Rocky IV* to make you squirm—except, of course, the acting, dialogue and plot."

I said, "This is why George Lucas movies do so well—there's not a thing in them about relationships. I'm no Lucas fan, but at least you know you won't have to watch a couple of Ewoks getting it on."

"Disney and Spielberg used to be safe, but now they're getting into high-risk areas. Ever since *Splash*, I've had to check out Disney.

Len added, "I'm even previewing plays now. Plays used to be safe, then I took someone to see *Glengarry Glen Ross* who was shocked I brought her to such a foul-mouthed play. I'd heard it was about real estate."

I asked Lenny if he'd rented *Twice in a Lifetime*, and he winced. "I wouldn't go near that with a 10-foot pole, much less a five-foot divorcée. It's about some guy who leaves his wife for a younger woman. I tell you, some of these movies can ruin a relationship."

"What I don't understand," I said, "is how teenagers can sit through teenage movies, which deal totally with sexual anxieties.

I still remember going to a Bergman movie with a date in college and breaking out in a cold sweat during *Wild Strawberries*."

"My theory about teenage sex movies," said Lenny, "is that boys and girls never go with one another. I made the mistake of taking a date to *Diner* and died a thousand deaths during the popcorn scene."

"If it's a foreign film it's never as bad," I added. "Sex isn't dirty in Swedish or Japanese, but if it's in English, with stars we actually *know*, it grosses me out. Ever since *Deliverance*, I've been trembling."

Nearing the box office, I said, "I think it's horrible that they release movies without warning grownups who may be on dates. There ought to be a rating that alerts adults to potentially embarrassing movies."

I said, "'B' could indicate a major scene that occurs in bed. 'K-13' might mean a kiss lasting longer than 13 minutes. 'MN' would stand for Male Nudity. 'WS' for Weird Sex, 'I' for Incest and 'O' for Orgasms."

"I always act very blasé during sex scenes," he said. "Usually, I'll yawn to express my profound boredom, or make a wisecrack to show that nothing fazes me. Inside, I'm a wreck. One woman wanted to see *James Joyce's Women*. I'd heard about the female orgasm at the end so I just said it wasn't as good as the book, *The G-Spot*.

I asked, "That takes care of sexual embarrassment but what about violence? Every woman I know hates violence and hides her face when the bloodshed begins. I know a woman who won't even see mysteries."

Len smiled. "This can work to your benefit. One other reason I check out movies first is to be on the lookout for scenes with horror and suspense—the scarier, the better. Before long, she's cowering under your coat."

"You sly devil! So what movies are safe for dates?"

"Don't miss *101 Dalmatians*," Lenny said. "I also recommend *Young Sherlock Holmes*, *One Magic Christmas* and, theatrically, most of Chekhov is OK. Of course, it does restrict your choices."

"No wonder people are renting cassettes now."

"It's ideal," he said. "You rent a film, pre-screen it and then ask a date home to watch, knowing there won't be any dirty stuff. That occurs later."

AN EXOTIC RETREAT CALLED HOME

THERE COMES A DAY in the life of every single when the best thing to do is climb back into your hole, like a groundhog who sees a shadow and decides it's nobody worth dating.

Such a day came recently to Doreen Dervish, my favorite would-be wild and crazy gal, who called to tell me she was entering one of her periodic dating retreats. It's like Main Chance; she calls it No Chance.

"I'm worn out," Doreen said. "I'm going out, but I feel I'm going in circles. I cannot bear to hear my life story one more time, much as it enthralls me."

"Just not meeting anyone interesting, eh?"

"It's not even that. I'm seeing a few guys, but the whole procedure has begun to grind me down. It's not the men, it's the *form*. It's almost more fun not to be at a French restaurant. I don't think I can look another stuffed trout in the face."

She added, "I get these mad cravings for a TV dinner. I love collapsing with the news, skipping a shower, eating canned chili and Dove Bars, watching *L.A. Law*, and just slinking around like a sloppy housewife."

"I know the feeling," I said. "There's nothing like not washing your hair to pep up a weekend. I often wallow in old newspapers for days, like a Tenderloin wino. Often, I just sit at my kitchen table thinking of all those smartly dressed dates driving around looking for some place to kill time after dinner."

"Exactly," Doreen said. "In fact, it's so much fun it's a trap. I've gone weeks like this, until I have to force myself to accept a date. I could become a nun with very little effort. I'm really into abstinence."

I smiled. "There's a lot to be said for desert islands. This is what happens if you go out too much. It sounds great in theory, but there's something just as appealing—almost thrilling—about deciding to stay home."

"Provided," she added, "it's your decision. If you feel like going out, and haven't a date, you're miserable. My unpopular and hermitry cycles never coincide."

I nodded. "It's sort of a singles midlife crisis—that burned-out feeling when every date begins to seem the same and marriage doesn't look half bad. It can be a dangerous state to slide into. Many people getting married these days are just sick of shaving on Saturdays."

"Or of the parking hassles," she said. "I hated my marriage, but I always had a great place to park. Plus, I didn't have to wonder whether to ask the guy in."

I asked Doreen what her favorite non-dating activity was. "Gee, there's so much to choose from. Mostly, I love knowing exactly where I'll be sleeping. I get an almost erotic kick out of sleeping with my old teddy bear. And he's always there for me in the morning."

I confided my own favorite monastic spree was being able to skulk around the house in a crabby mood instead of putting on a jolly dating face for five hours, non-stop. "I sometimes run out of peppiness by the time I pick up my date, and I need to sit in the car and pep myself up again for 10 minutes."

"That's what I like about my periodic retreats," said Doreen. "No need for jokes, no bright retorts, no groping for newsy topics and clever insights. It's so lovely being unstimulating for an entire evening. When you're home alone, the subject of abortion rarely comes up."

Doreen always know when she's about to enter a retreat mode. "I begin putting more and more days between dates, until pretty soon I've got a whole week that's clear and it's like a month in the country."

"How do you finally shake the dating blahs?" I asked.

"Well," she said, "after awhile the magazines and dishes start piling up, so I need an excuse to get out of the house. I know it's time to start dating again when my kitchen floor is stickier than an old movie theatre."

"Yeah," I agreed. "And one thing you have to say for eating in a fancy restaurant—they almost never run out of spoons."

"We understand each other pretty well," smiled Doreen. "Are you still in retreat?"

"I have been, lately," I said, "but spring is in the air. I'm about ready to emerge from my cave again."

"Me, too," she smiled.

"Well, look," I said, "if you're still free Saturday night . . ."

COMMITTED TO NONCOMMITMENT

M Y BACHELOR FRIEND Blincker just met someone he likes, and it's thrown him into a tizzy. He's terrified that she likes him.

Blincker has never been married, and whenever he senses himself approaching anything even approximating a committed state, he breaks out in giant splotches. Yet he insists he's not a confirmed bachelor.

"I don't know what it is," Blincker says. "I like Melanie but I already feel myself getting antsy."

"Ah, she's digging the ol' claws in, eh?" I said.

"Not at all," he said. "Melanie's not the type. We're not even close to anything serious, but already I'm nervous. I feel myself backing away." He shook his head. "I'm always looking for an emergency exit."

"You have what we at Singles Central call the Seven-Month Itch, or Pre-Commitment Stress, which happens to many single men the moment they pass that crucial six-month mark of dating somebody."

"It's not even two months yet," said Blincker.

I smiled. "The longer you're single, the sooner it occurs. I'll bet you first began to notice the sweat beads when Melanie asked what you were doing for Christmas."

"How'd you know?" he gasped. "You're uncanny."

"I suspect you're also afraid to call her too often, lest she think you're serious."

"Well, I am serious," said Blincker indignantly. "But I'm not, you know—*that* serious."

"How serious is *that* serious?" I wondered.

"More than casual but less than committed," he said. "I feel guilty if I don't call Melanie for two days," he said. "She doesn't say anything, but I can still feel those old guilt rays. They cut through steel."

"Are you by chance Jewish?"

"No, but I've *gone* with Jewish women, which is a partial conversion. I know what's expected of me."

"Maybe you're bringing this on yourself."

"I'm twitching all the time. I like Melanie a lot. I just don't want to get tied down. I'm not ready for it."

"But you're 35," I said. "How old is 'ready'?"

"I was thinking more in terms of 40," smiled Blincker. "That's a nice round comforting number."

"Sounds like you 'fear commitment,' as the ladies say."

"It gets worse and worse. At first, I just used to flee from marriage, then it was living together, then a steady relationship. Now

I'm sweating after three dates in a row. If a woman leaves a bobby pin behind, I figure she's trying to move in."

Blincker said, "Melanie suggested we go away for a weekend, but that has d. ngerous overtones. I'm not up for two-night stands. After 36 hours, I feel crowded. I'm afraid to sign a note 'love.' She may get some funny ideas. She's into cute cards. Lately, Melanie's been asking about my mother, often a dire sign. She's begun making dinners, and now she's talking about breakfast. It's very scary."

"You sure don't sound like someone who wants to find anybody, despite what you say."

Blincker said, "I'd like to be married but I don't quite know how to *get* there. If only I could wake up some morning and find myself sitting across the table from someone who said, 'Hi, I'm your wife.'"

I said, "You've got to quit thinking of marriage as 12,000 dates in a row."

Blincker sighed. "As soon as I like somebody, I start backing off. When I take out anyone new, I almost hope I won't like them, so I can say, 'Well, there's one more woman I won't be marrying.'" He threw up his hands, "I must be nuts! I'm almost at the point now when, if I fall for someone, I want to call it off before they fall for me."

"I think you're beyond saving," I told Blincker. "You really don't want to get married."

"I love the *concept* of marriage," he insisted. "It's the living together part that bothers me."

"Have you ever considered the priesthood?"

ROMANTIC RED FLAGS

SWEET. You fell in love but, between the twang of heart strings, there's something else, a wigwag signal—a Red Flag, the early-warning sign known to all wise hearts.

Beware the woman who: Writes cutesy notes, wears leg warmers on dates or jockwear to parties; gives sexual directions ("A little lower and then hang a sharp left"); watches *thirtysomething* but pretends to hate it; knows the 49ers by name; is "really into" anything (especially Windham Hill); uses "Ciao" or "Moi?"; has asymmetric haircut or visible tattoos; wears little white socks, Swatch watches or Reeboks; is a High Romance type who makes you feel like a Danielle Steel character.

Swoons over Mel Gibson, Richard Gere or Julio Iglesias; is tired of Woody Allen; has seizure if an old guy refers to "girls," disapproves of JAP jokes; says "You haven't called" (a death knell); mentions "Daddy;" wears bright green eye shadow; is a divorce victim; uses words like "bicoastal" or "networking;" has kids named Jason and Jennifer; orders Tanqueray and 7-UP; is reading Shirley MacLaine; swears by est, Weight Watchers or Scientology; keeps Kama Sutra oil, Nair or FDS in medicine cabinet; orders drinks containing pieces of fruit and rain gear; names car, plant or pet after Tolkien character; owns Doberman called "Nietzsche"; dyes hair a shade used by Coast Guard to find drowned airmen; has photo over bed of beaming parents; uses "relationship" on first date; knows name of bartender; suggests valet parking, or owns two or more cats.

The fun has just begun. Beware also any man who:

Wears a calculator watch, shirts in colors not found in nature, beer logo belt buckles, clothing made from petroleum byproducts or any T-shirt with writing on it; orders wine advertised on TV; reveals traces of brown rice or tofu in kitchen; has homemade cookies in jar (indicates girlfriend or Mom lurking nearby); owns shirts with contrasting cuffs and collars; has Helmut Newton photo book on coffee table and clear plastic frames on wall.

Plays only Wagner; keeps reptiles as pets; wears plastic pocket protector; has rotisserie, Lay-Z Boy recliner and Naugahyde furniture (has kids he hasn't told you about); keeps cat box in living room; owns smaller car than yours; undoes shirt below second button; wears Greek fisherman's cap; causes your dog to growl; wears visible socks; has unmade bed; rents furniture; overuses your first name like auto salesman; tells waiter, "We'd like chopsticks" without asking you; smells of English Leather, Jade East or Old Spice; is in PR.

Has pudgy hands; fails to turn down rock station when you get in car; is reckless or jerky driver (symptomatic of sexual style); has overdecorated apartment; carries beeper; chews gum; lovingly peels off one bill at a time; asks you to play Trivial Pursuit on first date; reads Michael Korda; has cellular phone; flashes Sears card; keeps tropical fish; owns Cuisinart with attachments neatly arranged in spotless kitchen; wears leather trench coat; has albums by Barry Manilow, Paul Anka or The Carpenters; goes to Tahoe for the shows; wears photo-gradient lenses.

Says "I'm a feminist"; has jungle-print sheets; wears short zip-up boots with little heels; makes more than one reference per date to ex-wife, Mom or last girlfriend; has tanning gel or Thorazine in medicine cabinet; wears Birkenstocks; names pets for opera stars; discusses "carbo-loading" and "Nautilus burnout"; carries Samsonite attache case with stick-on monogram; or says, "I want to be totally honest with you."

HELLO!
I'M VISCOUNT LINLEY

S URELY YOU KNOW the Marquess of Granby? Princess Ingeborg zu Schleswig-Holstein? How about the Duke of Atholl or Lady Silvy Thynne?

No? Such a pity. They're all terribly eligible, single and rich as Croesus, who is no longer eligible. Many are also cute. Most ski like madmen, disco and are just folks—equally at home in jeans or ermine, we are often informed.

They are but a few of the 80 aristocrats profiled in *Royal Singles* (Fireside, 1985). All are looking for Count or Countess von Right, but many will settle for a really neat commoner. Why not you? You could be the very one to sweep Contessina Francesca Braschi off her regal little feet.

Unquestionably, *Royal Singles* is where the major action is. After reading the book closely, I've decided to ask for the hand of Lady Amanda Knatchbull. What a doll. OK, she has a funny name, one of the burdens of royalty. Lady Amanda, 27, aside from being the granddaughter of the Earl of Mountbatten, knows Chinese and is a social worker. So she's also *nice*.

If Lady Amanda won't have me, there's Lady Helen Windsor, 18th in line, a "coltish beauty renowned for her phenomenal figure and called the royal family sexpot." Lady Helen smokes, but she could quit.

I'd even consider Marchesa Fiameta Frescobaldi, a tall, dark Italian beauty with big eyes who "does her best at whatever she tries, whether it's skiing or learning the family business" (count-

ing castles). And Baroness Francesca von Thyssen ("Chessie") is a knockout. Besides, her art collection is nothing to sneeze at.

I might give Jane Gilmour a call, except her father is a mere baronet and she lacks an actual title. Jane, a dish fit for a king, doesn't let that get her down: "She's closely connected to the highest ranks of aristocracy" but spends her time at parties. Foxy but bratty.

You might wangle an introduction to Lady Sarah Armstrong-Jones, Princess Margaret's 20-year-old daughter—not to mention Mum, who's forever available. Lady Sarah loves curry and frequents the Bombay Brasserie in London. Go for it!

On the way over, say hello to Count Manfredi Della Gherardesca of Italy, who works in his aunt's antique shop in New York, L'Antiquaire. You could mosey in, pretend to be looking for a 16th Century tapestry and when the Count walks over, ask him about Debussy or Keith Jarrett, two of his passions.

One of Europe's royal hunks would appear to be Count Johannes von Schoenborn Wiesentheid, 36, who is 6-foot-3, blue-eyed and tools around on a BMW motorbike or in a Cadillac convertible ("my pimp mobile," joshes Count Johannes) and lives in New Jersey, where he's a silversmith. He wanted to be pope, but left a monastery to go into banking instead. Hell, nobody's perfect.

A few singles I'd avoid are Lady Liza Campbell of Cawdor, who looks like an airhead (being descended from Macbeth and having "a deliciously engaging chuckle" isn't quite enough) . . . Lady Jane Wellesley, spurned by Prince Charles, she's fallen to "free-lance journalism" . . . Prince Karl von Habsburg of Austria (enjoys bobsledding, motorcycling and Charlton Heston) . . . Princess Margarita von Auersperg, who wants to be a secretary . . . Shah Reza, the shah of Iran's son, is in exile, always a strain on a marriage . . . and Catharine Oxenberg of Yugoslavia, the actress, is also "a keen boogie buff" but lacks a title and is 70th in line to the throne of England—a bit of a wait.

I'd also pass on Prince Nikolas and Princess Katarina of Yugoslavia (he digs trucks and bowling, she's a secretary who "recently added word processing to her skills" and works out to Jane Fonda tapes), and Lord Burghesh, who looks to be rather a twit.

Others to keep in mind: The Honorable Peregrine Moncrieffe, said to be a considerate date ("He'll order extra sauce on the side"); Prince Stefan-Leopold Zur Lippe of Germany, who studies law (nice to have something to fall back on just in case), likes rowing, asparagus and wants to be an astronaut (*First Prince in Space!*); Prince Abdulelah Al-Saud, who "has perfect teeth"; Princess Katya Galitizine of Russia, who eats mostly fruit; Prince Makhosetive of Swaziland, who can marry as often as he likes; and Scotland's Duke of Atholl, who is 52 but keeps a private army. After dinner, you can go review the troops.

Finally, you may want to check out the Dragon King, Jigme Singye Wangchuck of Bhutan, 30, who is "available at all times" and might consider settling down with an American gal. The Precious Ruler of the Dragon People doesn't do much but tour the country and talk to his subjects. Hey, it's lonely at the top.

MATCHMAKER,
MAKE ME A WINNER

I AM SITTING in the Cirque Room at the Fairmont Hotel await-
ing my dating service dreamboat.

I don't know what she looks like. We've only talked on the
phone, to establish the logistics of our half-blind date: a time and
place, preferably full of people and well-lighted, with security
guards.

Thus far, it looks like a date, it sounds like a date, but it does
not feel like a date. It feels like the night before surgery. It's my
fault, for enrolling in a dating service, which cost $100 for three
months; it's not unlike an apartment rental agency.

You fill out a form, listing what you're looking for, plus your
own sterling qualities, and are interviewed by a friendly young
woman, sort of a Yuppie Yenta.

The matchmaker and I meet on a Saturday morning on Post
Street in a tiny cubicle that she shares with an artist; there's a burl
clock on the wall and no heat.

She asks what I'm looking for. I spell it out, a subtle variation
on overall perfection. Will I go as far as San Jose for love? Sacra-
mento? Smoking or non-smoking? Any specific weight or height
requirements? Blue eyes or brown? What sort of hair? It's just like
picking out a puppy, or a baby.

Finally, one of many moments of truth: Pictures of the 30 Most
Semi-Wanted Women. A leatherette photo album is taken out, and
I thumb through it, trying not to look too anxious. It isn't difficult.

I examine Polaroid snaps of this female and that, in various
stages of social merriment, squinting at every feature, searching
for signs of intelligent life—a twinkle, a trace of charm, the
shadow of a smile. I see several group shots of people holding
drinks in badly furnished apartments.

Meanwhile, the Dolly Levi of Post Street tosses in encouraging asides: "She's *much* cuter than her picture . . . A good talker—I guarantee you won't be bored . . . That's an awful photo; she looks older . . . Oh, now she's adorable! This hairdo doesn't do her justice . . ."

As I leaf through the snapshots, fingers trembling, my heart sinks, for them as well as for me. It isn't the faces. It's that this whole thing is, at best, a shot in the dark—in the shadows, anyway.

Also, to be brutally frank, none of the faces looks especially promising. In real life, I would probably ask to come back when the photo exhibit changes. The woman who looks best (I learn later through a twist of fate) is no longer officially enrolled with the agency but her photo is still displayed. Dirty pool.

Reluctantly, I choose four possibles and exit, glad to be out on the street again, free at last, happily thrown back on my own modest social devices, no matter how chancy and clumsy.

Somehow, walking up to anyone on the street and commenting on the national deficit strikes me as a better plan than pointing to strangers in fuzzy snapshots.

A week later, the phone rings. Dolly says hello and gives me two names (I feel like a John LeCarré character), women who had studied my dazzling photo and are willing to risk it.

It seems that Laura—all names are changed to protect me—is a sales rep who calls herself "outgoing, understanding, friendly, fun, always there to help, with bangs and straight hair." Dolly tries to help me recall Laura, but it's futile; that was two weeks ago.

Contestant No. 2 is Chris, a "knee-jerk liberal with long red hair, quick, witty, kind, a risk-taker, charming, intelligent, a reader who digs Indian food and dogs."

After a week of stalling, I call Laura and am put off by the sound on her answering machine, a muzzy voice behind overly peppy music. Something too chirpy about her. I hang up, dial Chris and pray for a more enchanting answering machine.

Alas, a live voice answers and Chris explains, in a rapid-fire delivery, that she goes out a helluva lot, is "a fussy hussy" who moved here from Boston because she's "into the urban snap."

I shut my eyes and ask if she'd care to meet. "Let's talk first," she says, sounding like a dame out of Dashiell Hammett. "I want to hear how you put words together." The longer I talk to Chris, the more I crave Laura.

After talking by phone with my dating service dreamboat, I had a brief urge to remember a funeral in Alaska I needed to attend. There was something in the voice—a crass phrase, an over-wired tone, a wise-guy manner, a wish to sound hip and clever, all of which came into focus when Miss Match marched in the room.

Hedging our bets, we settled on a drink. We split after a polite hour of mutual apathy; I snuck several furtive glances at my watch. The main problem was how to part without sounding too happy or final. I breathed deeply, said, "Thanks for taking a chance!" in a jolly voice and beat a hasty retreat to my car, only to run into Miss Match in the garage. We both grinned like we'd seen a ghost.

A certain mystique, mingled with a lingering stigma, hovers over dating services. You figure anyone who signs up must be a desperate loser, with weird tendencies and green hair. Real people (you and me) find their own dates.

I used a modern matchmaker who works face to face, no computers, where all you have to go on are blurred photos and some dubious lines of self-description under categories like: What qualities are you most attracted to? What does "chemistry" mean to you? How would you describe your sense of humor? Identify yourself politically. How do you spend your leisure time? (After looking over my answers, I doubt if I'd go out with me.)

The photos tend to be fuzzy and forgettable by the time you're called by the yenta to announce she's got a live one. One thing about dating-service women, they have moxie and don't sit home a lot. It demands a gambler's nerve, humor and lowered expectations.

My dates didn't seem desperate, just adventurous. Of the three dates, one was a minor mistake and the others minor successes, easily as interesting, smart and lively as dates I might have arranged in my own hodgepodge style, made up of hopes and hunches.

Nobody arrived with more than one head and all had the normal number of left feet; both knew the mother tongue. Miss Match sounded wrong even by phone, yet I plunged ahead, intrepid reporter that I am.

All three dates were sight unseen, a risky plan, yet I could tell over the phone that even if someone turned out to be the Elephant Woman she'd be able to carry the conversation should I be struck mute.

As I awaited each date, I repeated the eternally irrelevant reassurance of parents through the ages: I wasn't going to marry the girl. Yet no matter how I prepared myself for the worst, I secretly anticipated fireworks.

Dates 2 and 3 fell short of even sparklers—matchmaking is an inexact science—but each was a credible human, smarter than expected. Yet even as I warned myself, I expected someone along the lines of Meryl Streep, or, at the very least, Holly Hunter.

There was a brief shock when neither of these fantasies appeared, then a second wave of relief that the person was actually pleasant looking and didn't cause me to race for the restroom between courses.

A woman I know, not named Myra, went on two dozen agency dates, and says they were all "fine." Myra retired in ennui. If "fine" is enough, rent-a-date is the answer. If, however, you're in the market for miracles, I'd advise approaching someone adorable in Macy's.

Myra, who is cheery, pretty and meets men easily, tried an agency because her would-be fantasy men turned into bums. "I was tired of going on instinct—seeing someone across a room." There's no future in handsome strangers. "I wanted to try an opposite approach, where looks and sex weren't involved."

After going on three dates arranged through the good offices of a professional dating service, I offer these conclusions: (1) They're not as bad as you think they're going to be, except when they're a disaster. (2) After 10 minutes, all mutual embarrassment wears off and it's just another date. And (3) Expect no miracles and be prepared for routine smalltalk.

The trouble with a dating service is that the all-important *click* is lacking, as it often is in life. In life, though, one begins with what seems like a faintly audible click and goes from there. Dating services are for people willing to forego, or delay, the crucial click.

In all three dates, I heard no clicks. There was nothing to push them over the top, no little spark, no Certain Feeling—the giddy first-date afterglow that sends one scampering to the phone the next morning.

CANNED APPLAUSE

T ODAY, SURROUNDED BY Thanksgiving with all the trimmings, I want to pause and recall those things that make life a bountiful feast for single folks who might otherwise starve. I speak of the waving rows of cans that line our land from shelf to shining shelf.

Let us give thanks, then, for the food that comes from cans, whose mighty harvest of chili beans, sliced peaches in heavy syrup 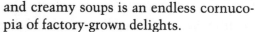 and creamy soups is an endless cornucopia of factory-grown delights.

Canned goods are real guys' fare. I am a longtime devotee of Campbell's soups, which, for many singles, are the staff of life; bread is a distant fourth, right after chive cottage cheese and Pinwheels.

Do you realize that a person could exist on Campbell's line of soups and never repeat himself in 50 years? And I'm not even counting Manhandlers.

Canned food gets no respect, not like your upscale frozen meals. Canned food is *not* lean cuisine; it is fat cuisine, basic grub—heat, eat and enjoy.

Canned food is simple and to the point. The directions rarely go over three lines, after which my mind tends to wander. "Add one can of water" is my idea of economical menu planning and tight writing; if it says "for added richness, use milk in place of water," I am already confused. Do I want added richness? Do I need it? Do I deserve it? If feeling wicked, I may add milk.

Frozen food is lovely but time-consuming. Your average single, who is either lazy or on the run, or both, cannot waste valuable seconds thawing out spinach crepes. Canned food requires no thawing, no microwaving, nothing but a can opener and pot. We're talking basic indoor survival techniques.

Maybe the nicest thing about canned food is it never improves or goes upscale on you. Oh, they may add "extra hot" or "chunky style" on the label, but that's it. If you haven't opened cream of tomato soup in 20 years, you will find no surprises, nothing new to grapple with—no clever pull tabs, plastic ribbons to unwind, no dotted lines or moving parts.

A can of soup still opens as it did in 1935 and the label looks the same (though I do miss the Campbell Kids). It has the same shape and feel. In fact, just scanning a shelf of Campbell's soup makes me feel hearty. I recall shelves from past lives, houses I lived in, frosted windows on wintry days. It looks all warm and cozy and, yes indeed, *mmm-mm* good!

Even when I don't mean to, I find myself grabbing a new variety of Campbell's soup, some of which I never actually consume (I still own an '82 can of cheddar cheese soup bought in a weak moment); it's pure reflex action.

I go through soup phases. One year, I devoured crates of cream of asparagus; another time I was heavily into tomato bisque. Currently, I am on a cream of potato binge. In winter, I lean toward cream of potato (chunk-style) or vegetable beef. I just like staring at the stuff simmering on the stove. Picks a fella right up.

For some reason, though, people are forever making cracks about canned goods, the Rodney Dangerfield of food. "If you only *knew* what they put in there!" health fiends warn. For years, I was afraid of fruit cocktail because of horror stories of what supposedly went on at fruit-canning factories—grisly tales involving weird sex acts amidst the diced peaches.

I still poke around in my dish of canned pears, to make sure nothing weird is swimming around in there, but I can report that, after thousands of dishes of canned pears and fruit cocktail, I've yet to find anything but what is depicted on the label.

Supermarkets hold me in awe, especially over the holidays, when they become a sort of mock grandma's house. The mere sight of a box of Stove Top Stuffing induces waves of nostalgia.

I am astonished at ongoing developments in cold cereals and cookies. Last week, I noticed that they've added raisins to Wheat Chex, which is something that would not occur to your average person. This week it was a mix of Shredded Wheat and bran; the combinations are astronomical. Even as we munch, some scientist at General Mills is working on a way to stuff a Cheerio inside a Rice Krispy.

Over at Checkerboard Square, they're doing remarkable things with nuts, apples, raisins and cinnamon, the four basic elements of cold cereal chemistry; chocolate has not worked out, happily. Too big a reach. Cookies is where all your major chocolate advances are being made these days.

Just when you think nothing more can be done with a cookie, along comes some Nabisco wizard who finds a way to coat a wafer with alternating stripes of peanut-butter and chocolate. Amazing. Gene-splicing is all well and good, but nothing when compared to the huge strides being taken at the Kraft, Kellogg and Nabisco labs.

ADVICE LIKE MOTHER USED TO GIVE

HARRY & EDNA'S IS a new service for single men and women that just opened, the brainchild of Paula Netwercker, whose agency is about to franchise.

"It suddenly occurred to me that I've been paying through the nose for the same stuff I used to hear around the house when I was younger—only then it drove me batty," she began.

"Do explain, for our listening audience at home," I prompted Paula, a keen woman of 32 summers.

"My folks, the aforementioned Harry and Edna, were forever on my back about meeting somebody, and I'd tell them to mind their own business. Then I started shelling out big bucks to total strangers to mind my own business."

Instead of throwing good money after bad for dating services, singles groups, classes, etc., Paula opened her own agency and hired her parents as in-house consultants, at a nominal fee.

"Clever concept," I said. "How does it work?"

"It's simplicity itself," she smiled. "When you sign up at Harry & Edna's, you're entitled to 12 months of constant badgering, what we call our Just a Little Friendly Advice for Your Own Good Package."

"Just what sort of advice?"

"All the usual parental nudging. Things like: 'Why don't you join a nice young people's group?'; 'Take an art class! Learn tennis! Go dancing!'; 'You'll never meet anyone if you sit in your room with your nose in a book!'; 'Don't think you're so special—everybody's in the same boat.' That sort of thing."

"It all comes flooding back," I said. "This could put the singles experts out of business in no time."

"What makes Harry & Edna's really work is that I charge $1,500. This immediately gives all of their homespun common-sense advice much more value than when your parents were dishing it out gratis."

"Could you reel me off a specific?" I asked her.

"Sure. Let's say you're sitting around moaning how hard it is to meet decent people. You see an ad promoting a new singles group that meets each week in a church social hall. When your Mom told you to go, you asked her to buzz off, but if it's a fancy outfit that charges a stiff fee, it seems an innovative way to meet people."

"What's the gist of your folks' advice?"

"It's a compendium of everything singles experts discuss at seminars: 'Don't expect the perfect mate to walk in the door,' 'A relationship is give and take,' 'If you want to find someone nice, don't be such a Mr. Critical—you're no Robert Redford yourself,' and that old standby, 'You need to make more friends.'"

"It sounds like a brilliant concept," I said. "I never thought of actually heeding my folks' advice."

"Of course not. Nobody did. Other people's parents always make more sense. What do you think the success of Dr. Ruth is based on, also Miss Manners, Abby, Ann Landers and Leo Buscaglia? They're telling you what your folks tried to drum into your head for 20 years but, oh, no, *you* were too smart."

Paula went on: "For instance, essentially Dr. Ruth says, 'Don't rush into sex.' Miss Manners says, 'Don't eat with your mouth full.' Dr. Leo says, 'Don't have such a long face.' And Abby and Ann say, 'Let your conscience be your guide' and 'Do unto others. . . .'"

"They really tell it like it is," I said.

"The problem with our parents was, they needed better writers and didn't know how to package themselves. They didn't go on talk shows, make cassettes or write syndicated columns."

"My folks didn't even tour," I said.

"Well, mine are penciled in for Donahue on the 17th," Paula said brightly.

"Tell me one thing—do your folks provide actual matchmaking counseling, too?"

"You bet," she said. "We're a one-stop agency. Dating is the bottom line. You show my folks a videotape of all the people you're dating and they tell you, in moments, which one is a bum, which looks like nothing but trouble, which one obviously is all wrong for you and which one is a lovely boy who is going to make something of himself. For a slight surcharge, they'll tell you the person you *should* marry, you should be so lucky."

"You mean Harry and Edna can tell me how to live my life *for* me, just like that? You'll make a fortune."

"Let's hope so," Paula said. "It's about time my parents' advice finally paid off."

"They sound like wise and generous people."

"They are," she said, "especially since I took over. I'm real proud how well they turned out."

SPEAKING WITH FORKED TONGUE

IN THEORY, the classic dinner date is a great idea, just the place to do all the serious sizing up that needs getting done, but most people think you can wing it.

The first date must be approached with all the care and precision of a job interview, which it often sounds like ("So, you've only been at this company six months, eh? Where were you before? What are your future plans?").

Eating and talking need to be choreographed so as not to interfere with each other. For example, never order pasta or anything that will end up dangling from your mouth as you compare cleaning women.

A spinach salad looks innocent but watch for giant leaves that unfold as you pull them from the bowl, like a magician's long silk scarf. Large salads are dangerous. Caesar's salad has a nasty splash factor to contend with. A tostada requires too much picking.

Crab Louis is a good thing to order because it lies there quietly. Cracked crab and lobster are out of the question, possible only for people who are already intimate. It's hard to conduct a serious conversation in bibs.

Stay away from things involving lemon, so as to avoid squirting someone during a longing gaze. Anything with tomato sauce is also asking for trouble, and I'd rule out all sandwiches and burgers. Leaking mayonnaise and catsup has spoiled many a tender moment.

Club sandwiches are a total disaster area. They not only drip, you can't get your mouth around one without looking like a ravenous savage. There's no way to give equal attention to a club sandwich and a funny story. The sandwich is going to win every time.

Never order anything you can't get in your mouth with a fork. Spare ribs is (are?) easily the worst idea for a dinner date possible.

I tend to discourage tricky items like escargots. They distract attention from *me* and, of course, leave lingering traces. Poached salmon is a safe, sane bet but only if boned. It's healthy, it stays on the plate and it's socially acceptable. *Bouillabaisse* is a bad idea. It smells bad, it splashes and you wind up with squirmy things dangling from your mouth. Ditto liver and onions and all Chinese food.

Veal is almost as wise (if boring) a first-date item as salmon. It's neat, it won't splash and it isn't red meat, but it's no longer politically correct either. Beef suggests you're a cold-blooded killer of innocent creatures and probably voted for Bush. Real women don't eat cows.

If you must order steak, make it as teeny as possible—tournedos, sirloin tips—so you don't spend the whole meal tearing into a slab of meat. A more liberal, stylish choice would be a nice cornish game hen—it's manageable and cute. All chicken is harmless, unless stuffed.

The original reason for nouvelle cuisine's popularity is that it appeals to people on first dates who appreciate its bite-sized portions. You can eat all nouvelle cuisine on a date without worry, because you don't truly care what you're eating and can simply discuss how lovely it looks.

Pizza is a high-risk meal. It doesn't show a whole lot of imagination, and it's difficult to look irresistible with mozzarella threads hanging from your chin.

Soup is harmless and most appetizers won't embarrass you, because they're tiny. Dessert is fairly foolproof, but dessert is also a personal statement. Keep it dainty. Giving in to chocolate decadence is fun but shows no inner resolve; bread pudding reveals grit and style. It's bad form to decline dessert and then eat half your date's *crème caramel*. This shows a sneaky nature.

A dinner date is rife with chances for you to make a solid impression or blow it. Did you get a good table? Do you hail the maître d' by name? Can you catch a waiter's eye with a flick of the finger? Are you adept at dealing with wine lists? If your meal is cold, do you sit there and groan about it, cause a scene or boldly send it back?

We come now to the delicate decaf issue. Poetic men order espresso; tough guys and swingers ask for coffee, black; rebels take tea. Decaf is for old geezers.

It's a rare man who can order decaf on a first date and not feel emasculated, but a sensitive woman never dwells on it. She says, "Hey, don't worry about it! It's very common, one cup of decaf doesn't bother me. It's *you* I like."

SHAKE UP THOSE STODGY DATES

A WOMAN FRIEND and I are working on a concept we've labeled Designer Dates: We plan your evening's entertainment, leaving you free to focus on the other person without being exhausted by logistics.

It is, after all, the nuts-and-bolts stuff that tends to wear you down and gives dating its logy, oftimes deadly, here-we-go-again feel, fretting that the dinner-movie combination you've put together is an uninspired cliché.

The inspiration for Designer Dating came from various directions. Someone told me about a recent date she'd had that was built around looking at Halley's Comet, which I agreed was a brilliant concept (if not comet), although she confided, giggling shrewdly, that it faltered in execution: "We never left my house."

This is fine. At Designer Dates, we encourage improvisation and only wish to sketch out the rough form of the evening while leaving the driving and/or snuggling to you. We want to leave enough slack in the evening for things like messing around and circling the block, although parking tips are part of the package—secret alleys, non-ripoff garages, faded red zones, etc.

If done right, the evening shouldn't look too planned. We want you to put your personal mark on each date. Ideally, of course, the date assumes it's all your clever doing.

Anyway, I decided to combine all these elements when the friend mentioned above told me, quite proudly, about a date she had artfully arranged that included a drink at Stars, a stroll through the Museum of Modern Art and dinner at the Hayes Street Grill.

"It went off beautifully," she reported, even though the museum part dragged when her date felt a need to analyze every painting. (I would say a museum is more like a fifth date, when you know somebody well enough to skip the entire Egyptian wing.)

To me, the best element of her date was that it was so geographically tidy. You only had to park once. The one-stop date is an ancient Grecian ideal. At Designer Dating, we also provide a sort of Trip Tik showing the easiest and quickest routes, with door-to-cafe driving times and scenic backroad cul-de-sacs.

No date will be suggested by us that hasn't been test-marketed and had less than a 90 percent success rate. All dates will be tried out first by a member of our experienced staff, to see how they work in practice. We hope to take the guesswork out of dating and do away with needless anxieties, allowing you merely to sit back and bask in the evening's proven merriment.

There are four basic plans. Nightlife Tour A is our First Date Starter-Upper and includes a chic-yet-undiscovered restaurant within your means where the maître d' greets you by name and whisks you to a corner table away from birthday parties and bridal showers.

It won't be the traditional, expected restaurant but somewhere sure to elicit wows ("What a *terrific* hideaway!"), followed by something totally unexpected, like comet-watching or clam-digging or—but I can't divulge more details. This idea is too hot to give away.

Nightlife Tour B is our Second-and-Third Date Combo offer, where we promise to top first-date excitement with a two-for-one sure-fire romantic evening. We pick a cozy place with a great view, probably involving a body of water (ask for our "Ocean View Bonus").

Tour B neatly segues into an offbeat but not embarrassingly stupid or boring film (you flash a card that gets you in without waiting outside with ordinary couples), or a comic who has been prescreened for raunchy content and who doesn't humiliate dates.

Nightlife Tour C is our Make-or-Break Date, where the purpose is to captivate someone who isn't sure if they like you. This appeals to people unable to move a relationship forward, or even backward. It calls for a certain zany aspect—something to loosen things up, perhaps a little hang-gliding, a visit to a mink farm and late supper at the all-new Popeye's.

Tour D is for old or ex-lovers, our Recapture the Original Spark Package, combining the highlights of tours A, B and C, concluding with a canoe ride that drops you off at your hotel, where you will stay for a magic weekend of round-the-clock laughs and sex. If interested, dial this toll-free number: 1-800-HOT DATE. (No salesman will call. May be slightly less fun where prohibited.)

ALL ABOARD FOR FANTASYLAND!

(The tale below is true except for two names.)

BARRY WAS A NEWLY divorced sculptor, 37, who was often called upon to speak to art classes at his alma mater, UC-Santa Cruz. He didn't do it for the fame nor, certainly, for the cash. He did it for the coeds.

It was Barry's fondest, oldest, fantasy that one of them would fall for him and pursue him madly after class to his lair. So far, however, he had only managed a few post-lecture flirtations and casual invitations to visit him in the city.

One Sunday at 11 A.M., six months after his last lecture, the phone rang and a cheery voice said, "Hi. This is Katie Mahoney. Remember? Last spring you talked to us in Mrs. Arnheim's art history class and, afterwards, you told me if I ever came to town to call." She giggled. "Here I am!"

Barry had no recollection of her, just a vague memory of offering one of his routine blind come-up-and-see-me-sometime invi-

tations that he passed around to coeds he eyed from behind the lectern. "I just can't place you."

"It's OK," she said. "I didn't think you would, but I sent you a note and a photo of me. Red hair? Freckles?"

"Uh, where are you, Kathy?"

"It's Katie, and I'm down at the bus station. I don't know the city at all. Do you think maybe you could pick me up? My girlfriend was *supposed* to be here."

Barry was thrilled but alarmed. "This is pretty sudden. Like I have plans . . . Maybe you could take a cab, and we could have coffee until you get hold of your friend."

"I don't have enough money for a cab."

"*Which* bus station?"

"I don't know the exact address. It's Greyhound. Do you have a map or something?"

He sighed, "OK, I'll be there. How'll I know you?"

She giggled. "Well, I have like a jillion freckles and I'm carrying a green knapsack. I'm in my grubbies."

On the way to the bus station, Barry tried to recall a freckled redhead in his fantasy past. When he pulled up, she was in blue jeans and had orange hair, and was sitting on a bedroll, squinting, looking only semi-cute.

He honked and she jumped in beside him. "Hi," she said. "You're real sweet to do this," and gave him a kiss on the cheek. "I'm so mad at Lisa. I don't know where she is. Nobody's at her house. I sure hope I have a place to stay."

"Yes," he said, making no offers.

"So where's your place?" she said. "I'd like to clean up before lunch or whatever. I feel so grungy."

Barry panicked. "I don't have time for lunch. Let's go somewhere for coffee and you can call Lisa again."

"Whatever," she smiled. "I have this awful feeling she's away all weekend with her boyfriend."

"So you have no money, no place to stay or any other friends?"

"That's about *it*, all right. If Lisa's not around maybe I could just stay at your place. I can sleep on the floor . . . anywhere. I've got my trusty bed roll."

"I don't think so, Katie. I have things to do."

"I won't get in your way. Honest. You can sculpt and I'll just like watch or sit and read your books, or watch TV."

"I know, but . . . " Back at his house, she brushed her scraggly hair and scrubbed her face; he expected to find a sink full of freckles. Barry said he had errands, just to get out. As he left, Katie was sitting crosslegged on the floor, studying his wedding album . . .

When he returned, her eyes lit up like a cocker spaniel. "I'm still here, as you can plainly see."

"Did you reach Lisa?"

"Yeah, but is *she* ever burned. Lis' claims I got the weeks mixed and that Jim is with her tonight. She says I never get anything straight." Katie began to cry; he patted her shoulder.

"Look, it's OK. You can stay here and tomorrow I'll give you money for the bus home."

"That's just it," she said. "I more or less ran away from home. I dropped out of school and had this big fight with my folks. I was coming up here to stay with Lisa."

"So you're literally homeless?"

"I guess so," she said. "What a bummer, huh?"

"A bummer indeed," he said. They had dinner at Uno's and groped for conversation. He learned that Katie was 22 and had dropped out of school four times. Afterwards, they went home and she vanished, then giggled from the back room, "I'm in your bed, as you can plainly see!"

It was only nine o'clock but, as there wasn't much else to do, they made love. Afterwards, she said, "That was so neat! I had such a fantasy of this. Didn't you?"

"Maybe," he lied. "So. What are your plans?"

"I guess I'll call my folks and like explain what happened and they'll have to let me move back in. Unless, of course, I can like stay with you a while . . . Could I?"

"No, no. You have to go home, make up with your parents and start school. You can't hang out here."

"I wouldn't be a problem to you. I know you have other . . . women, but I can get lost for a few hours."

"Why won't Lisa let you stay with her? She can't be mad forever. I thought you two were best pals."

"You'll *kill* me, but . . . there is no Lisa. I just made her up so I could stay here. I thought you'd like it."

"You made all this up?"

"Just like your fantasy. Except *I* made it happen."

"As I can plainly see," he said. "G'night." The next morning, he drove Katie to the bus station, dropped her off with $35 for a ticket and cab fare home, then drove away fast, before his fantasy chased him down again.

FOR A GOOD TIE, CALL . . .

V ERA SIMILITUDE, my much-married old friend, has just opened Dial-a-Mate, the ideal answer to men and women who, though needing each other in basic ways, are still not ready to settle down.

"Living together wasn't a real solution," Vera told me the other day over coffee on her sun deck—one of the many basic services of Dial-a-Mate, a round-the-clock agency that provides both crucial domestic data and hands-on help lacking in many lives.

"Dating is swell," she says, "but you can't ask a date to pick up some eggs for you on the way home. We're talking nuts-and-bolts domesticity. We supply everything but love and sex. If you want that, I'm afraid you may have to settle down."

"Sounds like the biggest advance in dating since the night-cap," I said.

"For instance, say you have a spot on your tie. Obviously, you tried to rub out a gravy stain and made a worse smudge. Why? Because you don't know the first thing about removing stains. One quick call to our Dial-a-Mate gravy expert would have given you the necessary *au jus* antidote. Just call 1-800-976-WIFE. We maintain a 24-hour spot-prevention hotline."

"Tell me more," I implored Vera.

"Let's say you're about to cook dinner and don't know how to sauté a chicken. You dial us and we have 35 skilled housewives  ready to take your call. No waiting. Just give your membership number and a sympathetic lady comes on the line to explain sautéing."

"It sounds like Triple-A road service," I said.

"Right, but we don't just dispense advice. You may need someone to come by and actually hang curtains, press a pair of pants or mend your jacket lining."

"How did you know?" I said.

"You seem the inept type. Call Dial-a-Mate and we send someone by who will not only hang your curtains but, if need be, also select the actual material and sew them, for which we add a slight surcharge."

"You must get all men signing up and no women."

"Don't be such a sexist," she said. "We get tons of calls from females who don't know a damn thing about curtains or chickens. I employ a staff of handymen to advise on phone jacks and leaky faucets, but single women are more capable at all this, so our neediest cases are guys. We are a full service firm, however."

"What do you mean?" I grinned wickedly.

"Not what you're thinking. Say you want to yell at someone but feel it's unfair to whine at a woman you're only dating. At

Dial-a-Mate, we send someone right over for you to gripe at for an hour. Or if you're rushed, you can just bitch by phone. I could even have someone at your home in minutes to nag you about your diet."

"This sounds like the answer to every single person's prayer," I said, "but what I need most is someone to do dishes and pay bills. I doubt such simple, tedious, ape-like tasks are within your bailiwick."

"How do you think I turn a profit?" Vera said. "We have check-writing and dirty-dish patrols roving the streets, equipped with two-way radios to respond to emergency calls from people who can't face another gas and electric bill or their 478th sinkful of dishes."

Dial-a-Mate's most popular service is a unit that not only de-livers breakfast in bed but, best of all, makes the bed afterwards. "We've got people who *only* want their beds made." She added, "Oh, did I mention our Hand-Holding Division?"

"Ah, and just what does that entail?"

"It's like the two of us here—having a chat over coffee. I have a crack team of highly trained moms who will swing by with oat-meal cookies and coffee, listen to your troubles, tidy up and leave."

"What does all this cost, pray tell?" I said.

"Depends," said Vera. "We have three classes of memberships: Terminally Inept, Incredibly Lazy and Occasionally Helpless. Or you can subscribe to our Total Helpmate Plan. This allows you ac-cess to our entire staff of willing schleps, on an as-needed basis."

"Well, maybe . . ."

Vera smiled and took out a form. "Look, why not sign up for a trial mate for 10 days, during which time we provide a woman who will come by each day and throw out the junk mail, make the cof-fee at night, pick out your tie and ask how it went at the office."

"Sounds lovely," I said. "I just don't know if I'm quite ready to commit myself that seriously."

THE JOYS OF SINGLEHOOD

ROM TIME TO TIME, I am taken aside and told that I am not positive enough about singledom. A good friend, a woman, chides me by saying, "You ought to give people some *hope* once in a while."

Well, hope has arrived. I don't know why it took so long, but, truly the news is not all bad. There's any number of goodies that come with being single, many of which are rarely discussed in polite company. We're among friends though, so here goes:

Lots Less Bickering: Apart from the occasional lover's squabble, being single is virtually bickerfree. No more ugly scenes on the way to parties, or coming home from parties; no more hassles about domestic minutiae; no more accusations that one is not listening, thoughtless or just not living up to one's potential. No more sour looks, long silences or disgusted sighs. The disgust level drops way below normal when you're single—assuming, of course, no children are present, in which case the disgust meter may soar to new heights.

Midnight Rambles: Living alone enables one to leap up at 11 P.M. and venture out for a cheeseburger. True, I have never done that, but if I ever *wanted* to I could, without having to (a) explain my behavior (inexplicable), (b) ask the other person to join me, (c) wake up said other person by mistake or (d) cause undue suspicions of a midnight tryst.

Crabby Moods: It is never necessary, as a single person, to wake up at 7 A.M. in a sweet disposition, or come home from work and launch into an animated discussion of the day's woes. You can growl at the world in general without feeling like a creep for being a grouch, thus adding to one's grouch quotient and creating a piggyback bad mood. Of course, having someone around to grouse at can brighten the day for some.

Burrowing in for Weekends: There is evidence that being single causes this hermit-like condition, but many people are born with basic hermit streaks that they need to curl up with. They want to be alone, and they don't want to have to list a lot of reasons. Listing reasons is a major burden of companionship. As one formerly married female friend once said, "You have to consult on *every*thing." When you're single, household meetings are few and far between.

Talking to Yourself: This misunderstood, and somewhat maligned, phenomenon is one of the little perks of single life. *You* know you're crazy but who cares? You can't very well prattle away to yourself with someone in the next room and not cause concern. Under the general heading of Talking, I include general profanity. I rarely converse with myself, but I do some of my best cursing solo, especially in the car, a veritable obscenity booth. I shock myself sometimes, but myself has heard everything and shrugs it off as the ravings of a harmless lunatic.

Eating Like a Pig: I don't mean pigging out, which is a well-known bonus of living alone and almost impossible to do with prying eyes around (one must sneak into the kitchen as if headed for the bedroom and cough loudly while opening the refrigerator door). No, I'm talking now about questionable table manners.

The decline of good table manners can be traced to a nation-wide rise in the number of people living alone and eating like animals. Singles may hold the fork any way they like, or not at all; they can eat ice cream out of a coffee cup and no eyes will roll. They may eat with their fingers, lick jam off their cuff, pluck a runaway raspberry off the floor and pop it in their mouth. They can bolt their food, leave their crusts, slurp their soup, play with their mashed potatoes—or spoon them directly out of the pot. One reason single people eat out a lot is to brush up on their table manners.

Weird Bedroom Outfits: I'm not talking about chains and leather boots. I have much grosser gear in mind—raggedy underwear, unmatching socks with holes much too threadbare for the Goodwill and, my personal favorite, promotional T-shirts unsuitable to be worn in public, not even covered up. I've tried it, but the logos show through your shirt.

My sleepwear includes shirts bearing the logos of Marine

World, the Child Abuse Council, KQAK, Alfa Romeo, the *Chronicle*, various trivia tournaments, a KQED ice-cream tasting and *Caddyshack II*.

Even if you've been married 25 years, I doubt if you can get away with this sort of stuff. Nothing is more likely to ruin your sex life than coming to bed in a T-shirt publicizing the KPIX Amateur Weatherman Contest.

SINGLES SURVIVAL KIT

UNBEKNOWNST TO MOST, singlehood is governed by certain natural laws every bit as formal and universal as the laws of physics. These we call "Nachman's Axioms," or Naxioms, a few of which follow:

First Law of Mixers: The enjoyment level is inversely proportional to the number of people in computer sales.

Second Law of Mixers: The best-looking women are always the ones taking tickets at the door.

Third Law of Mixers: The median age of any singles crowd is inversely proportional to the overhead wattage.

First Law of Hors d'Oeuvres: The ratio of cheese cubes and guacamole is one-fifth the amount of people huddled around the food.

Fourth Law of Mixers: The number of stockbrokers, minus the number of real estate agents, plus 2, equals the total amount of interesting men.

Fifth Law of Mixers: Last month's party is always better than this month's, by a factor of five.

First Law of Elite Singles Groups: The classier the name, the duller the club.

Sixth Law of Mixers: Beware of any invitation that says "jacket and tie suggested for men."

First Law of Networking: Never take out a woman who gives you her business card after one drink.

Second Law of Hors d'Oeuvres: Fritatta + gummy chicken wings disguised as drumsticks + pretzels + curry dip = a Fun Quotient of 14.

First Law of Guys: The scrawny men with frizzy hair and wire-rimmed glasses are the best dancers.

Seventh Law of Mixers: There's always a guy in a turban and he always makes out like mad.

First Law of Dating: Never date anybody with a funny recording on their answering machine.

First Law of Girls: Never get serious about anyone who says she's not looking to get serious.

First Law of Singles Bars: The age of people at any given singles bar is directly proportional to the age of the bar.

Universal Singles Law No. 1: Any couple eating lunch more than four blocks from the office is up to no good.

Second Law of Girls: Never make a pass at a woman who takes out her keys halfway home.

Eighth Law of Mixers: The most beautiful woman across a crowded room, when you get up close enough to say something, always has her arm around the guy next to her.

Second Law of Guys: Jerks tend to travel in packs of four or more.

Universal Singles Law No. 2: Never get involved with anyone who lives with two or more cats, owns a water bed or doesn't drive.

Second Law of Singles Bars: According to the Nachman Curve, the major drinkers congregate at the near end of the bar, bores at the back and the newly divorced toward the center.

Universal Singles Law No. 3: Never go out with anyone who watches *Dynasty*, reads USA Today or has a bumper sticker incorporating any of these phrases: *"I brake," "whales," "nuke"* or *"—do it . . . "*

Third Law of Singles Bars: Never go out with anyone who slams down a dice cup.

Universal Singles Law No. 4: Never date anyone who lives in a houseboat, on a cable car line, in the Berkeley hills or on an unmarked road in Mill Valley, no matter how damn cute they are.

Third Law of Girls: Never get serious about anyone who wears leg warmers to dinner.

Ninth Law of Mixers: Avoid strangers who spend all night making phone calls.

Fourth Law of Girls: Women who write in green ink are the same ones in college who dotted their i's with happy faces.

Tenth Law of Mixers: If you haven't danced by 10:20, you won't.

RING ON HER FINGER, MEN AT HER FEET

I RAN INTO Nora Evergreen, my always-a-bridesmaid friend, and expected to hear the usual lamentations for the single woman. Nora considers herself the most unmarried person who ever trod the earth. Instead, to my astonishment, she held out her left hand and revealed a gold band.

"Congratulations!" I gasped. "You finally did it!"

"Well, not quite," she said, "but my social life picked up the moment I began wearing this little bauble."

"You mean you're *not* married?"

"I'll explain," she said. Over coffee, Nora told me of the ploy she had devised for attracting single men, a discovery worthy of the Nobel Prize for chemistry.

"It's simplicity itself," she said. "I just went out and bought a wedding ring, and suddenly single men were throwing themselves at me. It's built on the premise that singles think all the best people are married. Also that single women are taken for granted, except by married men, while married women are special—to single men."

Nora got the idea from a married friend, who told her that a surprise benefit of marriage is the ring itself.

"She was so right. Now, I can walk up to any man and talk about anything. I'm non-threatening. I can even tell dirty jokes I couldn't before. In the eyes of many men, especially older ones, the ring makes me legitimate and respectable. This is useful in dealing with salespeople, mechanics and men in the office, some of whom look at young unmarried women with faint suspicion, assuming either they're tramps or lesbians. I can't imagine not wearing a ring again."

"What you're suggesting," I said, "is that the gold ring, aside from its symbolic, romantic and spiritual meaning, also has vast built-in ego-boosting powers."

"Exactly," she said. "As soon as I slipped on this ring, it was like putting on Wonder Woman's magic belt. I lost all my inhibitions and fears. I cast off my old worries as a single female. I felt less conspicuous, less judged, less vulnerable and much more exciting."

I asked Nora what happens if she meets someone who wants to marry her.

"It happens all the time now," she smiled. "That's the whole point. I'm in great demand."

"Sooner or later, won't you have to explain?"

"No problem. Once I've got a guy's attention, I just say the ring belongs to my late twin sister, or that I only wear it to frighten away creeps."

"So you're hot now," I said.

"Very. For a single man, a married woman is the hottest thing going—forbidden fruit, you know."

"Don't you feel you're being a bit . . . unscrupulous?"

"Not at all. I know single men who wear wedding rings as a way to avoid a serious relationship. I'm wearing a ring to find one. It invariably catches their eye. Men always want what they can't have."

"Isn't there a slim chance that a man, upon hearing a woman is in fact single, will feel a mite manipulated?"

"I withhold that news until the proper moment—after the man falls desperately in love with me and insists he must have me, regardless of my marital ties. Then I fling off the ring. If I'm unsure of a man's true feelings, I concoct a phantom husband. Mine is named Jeff. We've been married six years. No kids."

"Tell me more," I said.

"When Tony, my fiancé, fell for me," she said, "I just lowered my eyes and told him, 'I love you very much, Tony, but I can't leave Jeff. He depends on me.' This made me seem doubly desirable. Tony pleaded with me to leave Jeff and kept making extravagant promises about our future together."

She added, "So I twisted my ring and said, 'I just can't do this to Jeff; he'd be devastated. To him, I'm the sun, moon and stars. He left a gorgeous young wife for me.'"

To flesh out her story, Nora bought a Woolworth frame with a handsome movie star photo and said it was Jeff.

"Tony got suspicious and wondered why Jeff looked like William Hurt. I said, 'Everyone mistakes them, but Jeff's taller and his body is better.'"

She laughed. "It make Tony insanely jealous and unsure of himself, knowing he was up against such a devoted hunk. He tried even harder to win me. Finally, I agreed to break the news to Jeff and left him for Tony."

"How did you explain to Tony your lack of domestic quarters and joint belongings?"

"I told him I let Jeff keep everything in exchange for my freedom. I even let Jeff have the dog and the VCR. I said it was worth it to me to be with him always."

Now Nora and Tony are almost one, except that ever since their engagement he's been less attentive, but she's found a way to keep him interested:

"I just write myself impassioned letters from poor distraught Jeff, begging me to come home. It works miracles. Speaking of which, I hope you can make the wedding."

NO DANCING
ON THE DESKS

I T IS NEVER TOO early to begin shopping for a date to the office Christmas party, a slight contradiction in terms. Making jolly chitchat with people whom you know either too well or only as hallway figures requires new powers of invention, if only to avoid asking the controller, "So what do you do around here?"

The office-party concept is more than a little dicey. It's tricky enough if you're married. If you're single, the annual Christmas party assumes distinct socio-political overtones, rich in subtext and nuance.

You can't take just anybody to the office Christmas party. It is vital to bring the socially correct date, hopefully someone who will cause a nice little ripple and, ideally, popping eyes.

Couples have no choice, so it's up to the unmarried pool to provide grist for gossip, speculation and next-day chuckles.

If you're single, you need to bring someone who (1) looks fabulous, (2) will charm the boss' socks off, and (3) does not engage in untoward behavior, under which falls Getting Smashed, Dancing with the Office Jerk, Flirting with Mail-Room Boys and Saying Stupid Things About the Firm.

At our own Christmas party, such examples of the latter would include: "I just don't have time to read a newspaper," "I never remember, is the *Chronicle* the morning or the evening paper?" "Why can't I ever find Jumble?" and, "I gave up the paper when you dropped Gordo."

It is smart to take one's Best Girl/Guy to the office party, someone you can count on to dress respectably (no miniskirts, gold chains, crazy headdress or see-through blouses) and make engaging banter.

The office party is primarily a family affair, about a PG-13, but it's also the place to show everyone you're not the drone they take you for, by bringing a hot date, if only to shake things up and give everyone something to chortle about over lunch the next day, when the entire party is pulled apart, couple by couple.

It's almost more important to be present at the *après*-party dish session, rivaled only by teenage sleep-overs for sheer ugliness.

The office party casts colleagues in a new light by bringing mates out into the open for the first time. Unlike most parties, everyone knows you and is watching like hawks—buzzards, rather—to see what sort of a social animal you are and how your personal life jibes with your office persona.

Executive swingers suddenly appear with mousy mates, wimps turn up with Tugboat Annies in tow, the newly-divorced bring mail-room girls and Xerox machine Alexis Carringtons arrive with paunchy husbands.

This isn't just a date you're making, it's a statement. Also, it may be subtle signal to the date her/himself, who is likely to read implications into this seemingly innocent event. Taking someone to the office party is only a step or two from bringing them home for Thanksgiving.

By the same token, if you bring a VIP date to the office party, fellow workers must not make fools of themselves in front of you; this includes asking for your date's card when you're at the punch bowl.

Colleagues should laud you loudly, saying things like, "Hey, we'd be in Chapter 11 if it wasn't for ol' Diane here!" or, "Chet's the sweetest guy in the office—all the women have a thing for him."

Be careful whom you talk to, taking care to avoid office jesters who enjoy getting off droll comic remarks like, "Hey, you ol' rascal, which one is this?," "Well, she must be that hot number we've been hearing all about!" and, "So, ah, Roy, where's the Missus tonight?"

I REWRITE THE SONGS
THE WHOLE WORLD SINGS

WHETHER SAFE SEX should be introduced into contemporary rock songs is an issue still tearing the music industry apart. A more urgent question than harmless Beastie Boys tunes, however, is what to do about the *old* songs—and also who should be the guardian of lyrics where the damage is already done.

I suspect I'm the only man for the job, repugnant though it is. We here on the Dirty Old Songs Board are concerned about tunes like—I blush to repeat them in print—"I've Got You Under My Skin," "I'm Just a Girl Who Can't Say No" and "Let's Do It."

These songs are far more dangerous than heavy metal hits because you can understand the lyrics. Such songs are responsible for untold millions of unwanted children.

Enough damage has already been done, but just in case these songs should be heard by young people used to innocuous Johnny Rotten songs, they need revising.

Removing them from the air is censorship. They're barely on the air anyway, yet you can't be too cautious. Some innocent young girl could be stuck in an elevator and overhear the words to "The Nearness of You" and get in trouble.

Many people are concerned, lest younger—or worse, older and more susceptible—listeners take some of the lyrics too literally.

With a blatantly suggestive number such as "I've Got you Under My Skin," we have no choice but to change it to:

"Before I've Got You Under My Skin Maybe We Better Talk About It." Or, "I've Got You Under My Covers and Walgreen's Is Closed."

Our committee's alternate suggestion, "I've Got You Under My Lambskin," was nixed as more suggestive than the original lyric.

The funny Rodgers & Hammerstein ditty from "Oklahoma!" doesn't quite work as "I'm Just a Girl Who Can't Say Yes." There may be a middle ground, such as, "I'm Just a Girl Who Can't Say No, So I've Brought Adequate Precautions." It might even be repackaged as, "I'm Just a Girl Who Can't Say No Except to Drugs."

As for "Let's Do It," the only possible rewrite is, "Let's Sort of Do It," or perhaps, "Let's Do It After We've Had a Talk." Songs like "Let Yourself Go," "Do, Do, Do" and "You've Got That Thing" have no foreseeable future, and "Body and Soul" probably has a limited appeal as "Brains and Soul."

"It's All Right With Me" needs to be banned from the air, what with its risque lyrics:

"Though your lips are tempting, they're the wrong lips. / They're not her lips but they're such tempting lips / That if some night you're free, / Dear, it's all right, /It's all right /With me."

Dangerous stuff, unless that last phrase could somehow be rewritten to read, "It's all right with me, / If you tested negative and germ free." It doesn't quite scan but it's clean.

Cole Porter's "All of You" is as decadent as anything Frank Zappa ever wrote, and the part that goes, *"I love the looks of you, the lure of you, / I'd love to make a tour of you, / The eyes, the arms, the mouth of you, / The east, west, north and the south of you,"* ought to be revised to:

"I love the looks of you, the lure of you, / I'd love to make a tour of you, / But first I better be sure of you . . ."

Certain songs, though they needn't be rewritten, are bound to be affected by the new morality and suddenly take on new, rather forlorn and nostalgic meanings:

"Isn't It a Pity?," "By Myself," "There's a Lull in My Life," "This Can't Be Love," "Fools Rush In," "Blues in the Night" and "What's the Use of Wond'ring?"

"Anything Goes" has lost all meaning, and there are new ironic overtones to "I Get Along Without You Very Well," "Why Can't I?" "Imagination" and "Where Is the Life That Late I Led?"

Many standards, on the other hand, are likely to enjoy a new popularity, numbers like: "You Better Go Now," "Give Me the Simple Life," "Let's Have Another Cup of Coffee," "A Fine Romance," "I Guess I'll Have to Change My Plan," "Make Believe," "Taking a Chance on Love," "They Say It's Wonderful," "Luck Be a Lady" and, of course, "Getting to Know You."

SEX AND THE SINGLE COLLEGE BOY

W E HAVE A NEWS item here about the fact that male college freshmen engage in twice as many sexual fantasies as new coeds.

This does not square with what I had been led to believe in college, that "girls think about it just as much as guys."

That was an encouraging rumor that went around in those days and, I assume, continues to go around. Or did until this survey was published, dashing hopes on campuses coast to coast.

When I was a freshman, the concept behind this fantastic notion was to set the male mind at rest, in case you thought maybe there was something wrong with you—that you were, well, "oversexed." Has the definition of "over" ever been precisely determined?

You would get to talking with a few of the guys about girls and some expert would say, "Listen, girls think about it *more* than guys—you better believe it!"

I certainly did not believe it, nor did I want to believe it. Nothing in my own paltry experience led me to believe that women ever thought about sex; not around me, anyway.

I couldn't imagine anyone, especially a girl, having more sexual fantasies than I did. I couldn't even imagine another guy having that many.

It troubled me to realize that women even *had* such fantasies—urges, yes, OK, but not actual fantasies, with costumes and props and backlighting. Girls might dream about sex, but that was different (they couldn't help what happened when they were asleep), but conscious fantasizing? Please.

At the time, of course, I wasn't having what you could call major sexual fantasies, what with so little to work with—Lois Lane, Sheena: Queen of the Jungle, Debbie Reynolds, the Doublemint Twins, Wonder Woman.

That was it, boys. If you craved fantasy, you had your work cut out for you. Today's college guy has it too easy. When I was a lad, *we* had to trudge 10 miles through the snow to get to a decent fantasy.

Sexual fantasizing has made some hefty advances since then, back in the ice age before Marilyn Chambers and "Letters to Penthouse," when college boys' fantasies consisted of getting a date with the homecoming queen. Or anyone.

No, that's wrong. The idea of a date with the homecoming queen was beyond fantasy—it was idiotic. Even as a fantasy, I couldn't buy it.

A much more reasonable fantasy was getting the homecoming queen to smile at you in the bookstore. Our homecoming queen worked in the bookstore, which stunned me. The idea of royalty having to earn her tuition like a common pompon girl was barbaric.

My major freshman fantasy was imagining myself speaking to the homecoming queen, and then—get this, guys!—having her . . . answer me. The fantasy went thusly:

Me (*shyly but with feeling*): "Gosh, Cyndi, you're much cuter than your picture in the *Daily*."

Homecoming Queen: "Oh, aren't you nice! What's *your* name?"

The rest of the scene has sort of faded, but I could live on that for weeks.

This survey of campus sexual attitudes—taken by a woman at the State University of New York—asserts that freshmen average nearly eight sexual fantasies a day against 4.5 for freshwomen.

I should think eight per hour is more like it, spread out fairly evenly over the girls in History 17A.

The news story says: "(Researcher Jennifer) Jones' study did not address the content of the fantasies or explain why men had more fantasies than women." Let me address it, since Ms. Jones obviously is too shy.

Is it that men have nothing else on their minds, or that women have less fertile imaginations, or that men are merely more wanton creatures?

No, the two reasons are, first, that men have to think about sex more, to bring the girls up to speed. If college women would stop dreaming about careers, and start fantasizing more about sex, a lot of these college guys could relax.

Second, all the frosh coeds are dating juniors, so freshmen have nothing else to do but sit around and think about it.

DR. SINGLEBERG WILL SEE YOU NOW

(Dr. Meyer Singleberg, the not-quite-renowned relationship doctor, has agreed to answer questions from his anxious unmarried public.

Q. Doc, I'm worried about my lack of meaningless encounters. Due to anxiety over this-or-that disease, I feel I could become accidentally involved in a long-standing relationship that is based less on mutual trust and respect than fear and loathing.

A. The one-night stand is a fling of the past. Even one-month stands are in decline. Long-term relationships are the only safe ones, with marriage the safest of all sexual encounters—almost too safe, in many cases. If you make love with someone, you better marry her, just like in the old days, a nostalgic return to the '50s and monogamy and outdoor barbecuing.

Q. Why does every woman who's single own a cat? Is this a coincidence? Is there some deep-seated psychic need or do girls just wanna have cats?

A. Yes and no. It's not quite so simple. A dog cannot take the single life. The lifestyle is too erratic. All the highs and lows give dogs ulcers. Dogs are family. They need patting, like wives. A cat is able to subsist for weeks with a couple of nuzzles behind the ear and a toy mouse. This will only satisfy a dog for two minutes.

The cat is better suited in every way to live with a single person. Everything about the lifestyle appeals to it—the independence, the weird hours, the litter, the peculiar feeding times, the incessant grooming. A dog tends to go nuts. He can't understand why the so-called man or woman of the house is never home—and, when they are home, is puzzled by all the strange people trooping in and out in the wee hours of the night. A cat, being a nocturnal animal, isn't bothered by people creeping about in the dark, but it spooks out a dog. A dog wants to know what's going on. A cat can go with the flow.

Also, a cat doesn't mind the long empty hours that are part and parcel of the single life, the lonely weekends and neglected nights. Being cooped up for days slowly drives a dog bonkers; a cat enjoys just sort of lazing around in the sun, getting a great tan.

A dog needs to get out. On the other hand, many fine relationships have begun by walking one's dog. Similar results have not been reported by people walking their cats. While many consider being single a dog's life, in fact it's a cat's life. Your average cat understands. Its laid-back, unflappable little biorhythms are more in synch with the single psyche. This explains such romantic expressions of approval as "You're the cat's whiskers!" (meow, pajamas, etc.). Just about the worst thing you can call a single person is a dog.

Q. My boyfriend refuses to let me see the inside of his house.

We always have to go back to my place. He says his house is not safe for women and children.

A. Your boyfriend is typical of males afflicted with "home-ophobia," or the dread of women moving in. Many women have never seen the inside of their lovers' homes, except when it goes on the market. Many men harbor irrational fears that if a woman is allowed in their home for 36 hours, or one weekend (whichever comes first), she'll slowly build a nest, one bowl at a time. Single men report the sudden appearance of new shower curtains and plants. One such fellow awoke on a Monday morning and said, "Hey, that cat wasn't here yesterday."

Q. Very often, when I ask somebody out after meeting her at a party, she doesn't look as good when I pick her up. Can I avoid this letdown?

A. You refer to a dating phenomenon called "before-glow," when the spark of that first encounter burns away a week later. To keep the magic intact, go direct from your initial meeting to Paris.

Q. At parties, I never know how long I'm suppose to talk with someone. I can't tell when my date wants to leave.

A. Just say, "May I please go now?" A good time to leave is when you notice that the person you're talking to is sneaking looks over your shoulder at someone else—rude but normal singles behavior, searching for someone cuter just around the next canapé. Always carry two drinks and say, "Sorry, but I *must* deliver this."

Q. What's with all these guys who tell you they'll call and never do? How long should I wait for a man to call?

A. A man who says he'll call and doesn't is considered legally dead, or missing in action, after two years. There are reports, though, of women receiving calls from men after as long as eight years, explaining, "I've been tied up with work." When a man says he'll call and doesn't, either (1) *He has lost his nerve* (Most men's nerve vanishes upon reaching their cars); (2) *He has lost your number* (never use a cocktail napkin or business card; write it on his forehead); or (3) *He has lost interest* (the average interest span of a single man is 17 minutes, 4.5 minutes for married men).

Q. Some men consider the one-night stand still acceptable, herpes or not. Are these guys crazy or what?

A. Many guys still propose a one-night stand one so they won't seem unmanly, knowing full well no sane woman will accept. This way, a fellow can look macho while making *you* feel like a pill for saying no.

Q. Why do some women think that, if you sleep with them, they have telephone rights in perpetuity?

A. For some women, calling the next day is part of the sexual act. In many cases, the best part.

Q. I have trouble sleeping with women—literally. The sex part is a cinch. It's all the cuddling that wears me out. Most women I know are cuddle fiends and want to hug all night, turning me into their cuddle slave. I can't get a few winks. Or else they sleep all over the bed. How do I let someone know she's welcome to stay but that I need my space?

A. Hogging the bed is the third major cause of singleness, right after smoking in bed and gambling in bed, and a big reason many people never marry. One way of dealing with the situation you describe is to draw a double yellow line down the middle of the bed and then glue onto the mattress a few raised highway bumps so that, even asleep, the other person will sense when he or she is inching into your lane.

Another possibility is the break-apart box spring. A third way, devised by Rube Pavlov, is to wear a beeper to bed. When Person B sneaks into Person A's territory, buzzer stirs B, causing A to gingerly nudge B to far side of bed.

Q. When I want to tell a woman she's beautiful or sexy or cute, I can't find the words—or rather, I can't say the words. I have a dread of sounding like a Rod McKuen song or some drip out of Rosemary Rogers. There's no way to say, "You're breathtakingly beautiful!" or "You're the sexiest woman on God's earth" without cracking everyone up, me included.

A. A common enough concern, but the trouble isn't in the language—it's finding the proper tone of voice. You might want to work at home with a tape recorder and a mirror, to check facial expressions. One wants to sound sincere yet not sappy, overcome but not overblown. Since she's heard this song before, one must sound personal, genuine and totally unrehearsed.

If you say she's the loveliest creature God ever put on earth, and your voice is all wrong, you've had it. If you tell her she's "more alluring than Kathleen Turner," she'll be suspicious, and with good reason—nobody uses works like "alluring."

A few other terms to avoid: "exquisite," "ravishing," "swell," "smoldering," "sublime," "limpid," "neat-o." Terms such as "pretty" and "sweet" and "charming" have lost all meaning. "Beautiful" still packs a wallop, unlike "pretty," a near slur. Avoid "marvelous."

Q. In the throes of passion, my boyfriend insists on hanging up his trousers and shirt, rolling up his socks and putting his shoes neatly in the closet. I find this a real turnoff. It breaks the mood for me and prevents me from achieving, you know, the Big O.

A. Many people find flinging their clothes about is the most exciting part of the entire sex act (or in some cases, skit), while others find the actual hanging up of trousers and skirts to be incredibly erotic. I can only quote you the inscription over the entrance of the Singleberg Relationship Clinic: *"To each his own, to forgive divine."*

Q. After a night of wild sex (OK, 25 minutes), is it unromantic to remake the bed before going to sleep?

A. It does take some spontaneity out of the event to flick on the light and redo the bed at 3 A.M., but some people find it hard to sleep with pillows on the floor, the sheets in a granny-knot and a quilt in their mouth.

Q. I find myself going out with terribly attractive women even though I know they're dull. Is there any way to break myself of this ugly habit before I die?

A. So far as we know, mind-numbing dates are not life-threatening, but I would suggest six weeks at Last Chance, our ranch in the rolling hills of Bolinas, California. At Last Chance, which combines the principles of est and life itself, we provide you with dozens of routine-looking people who are smart, funny and interesting. For six weeks, you undergo a strenuous dating regimen, with only occasional breaks to go to the bathroom; you may make only one phone call, to your service.

Q. I find myself falling asleep on dates, usually while our waiter is nattering on about the monkfish in peanut sauce, or as I'm driv-

ing somebody home. **Is it nerves or am I truly as bored as it must look? Also, what the heck is a monkfish?**

A. I'd say you've got dateolepsy, where, for seemingly no reason, you grow drowsy by 8 P.M. There are rare cases of people actually falling face down into their cream of monkfish soup, a victim of "yawning gaps." This afflicts otherwise healthy single men and women whose brains, in a fevered attempt to fill long silences, are suddenly deprived of oxygen and subject matter.

A monkfish is a selfless flounder whose quiet life is devoted to serving yuppies.

SOME DISENCHANTED EVENINGS

WHATEVER HAPPENED to Romance?," Adair Lara wonders in a recent article in which she despairs of the modern man's approach to wooing. "There's no fateful encounter, no mist, no roses, no proposals," sighed she. Obsessive love died with Edna St. Vincent Millay.

The modern Galahad, it seems, is too pragmatic. Forget fateful encounters. Strangers locking eyes across a crowded room occurs only in old musicals, replaced by paid-for encounters—personals, singles bars, blind date agencies, clubs for non-smoking skiers.

Intimate dinner, she says, means splitting the tab or the man preparing it himself, to flex his female muscles. There's no time for sonnets when it's more important to discuss the relationship, charting its progress like a hurricane. Passion has been reduced to midnight seminars, with frank discussions by lovers clutching pamphlets and flow charts under the covers.

Allow me to put Ms. Lara's fears to rest (if not to sleep) and try to explain the plight of the modern romantic man. We're out here, kid, but we've been browbeaten into submission by the hip Anti-Romantic Mafia.

The cool mob took over right after *Love Story* (where drippiness replaced good honest longing) and made it tough for romantics to operate in our former assured old-fashioned semi-crazed way, for fear of being considered corny and unhip. The trouble, of course, is that love is uncool.

Wiser, harder heads prevail today when your own foolish mushy head wants to prevail. You fall in love and everyone tells you to go easy. "You'll frighten her away," they say. "I'd soft-peddle it for now."

If you send flowers, you may insult her delicate feminist sensibilities in some way. The New Woman does not want flowers— she wants comparable pay, so she can buy her own flowers. Anyway, flowers are sexist and candy contains sugar. Let *her* send roses.

You feel like taking a moonlit drive in the mist but suspect she'd rather be dancing to Motley Crüe at the Oasis, where girls just wanna have fun.

You'd suggest going to your place and listening to some Sinatra, but Sinatra is politically incorrect, also dated, the very essence of macho. Worse, the old songs have been discredited as a sham. Stevie Wonder and Billy Joel aren't quite the same thing. There's still Linda Ronstadt, who made old love songs semi-respectable for a few hours.

Romance was never easy, but the modern romantic male lost heart, which was pretty faint to begin with. In the old days, it was all he could do to write a love letter; today, he sends a funny card to cover his tracks or leaves a clever message on her machine. The only moonlit canoe trips now are sponsored by singles groups.

Chance encounters are unreliable, even dangerous, which is why they're so wonderful. According to studies, love at first sight is nonsense and probably an indication of some deeper disturbance. Research shows that such romantic yearning is caused by a lack of phenylethimanine—a temporary chemical imbalance, which we all knew, only it used to go under the name of being swept off your feet.

Of course, the true romantic isn't daunted by all that. The problem is that romance today is suspect even as a concept. Too many Peter Pans and Dance-Away Lovers around. No follow-through—or, in Ms. Lara's words, "no proposals." Romance has been abused. So forget the moonlight-and-roses, buster; let's see a prenuptial agreement.

Maybe it's just the same old romantic trying to please in new ways. To stay current and maintain his dignity among the skeptics, the modern romantic forgoes a box of candy for a boxed set of Ann Beattie.

Intimate dinners now need to be the right cuisine at a four-star place you probably can't get into (and if you do, is too noisy for sweet nothings to be heard). Before you fall in love over a candle-light dinner, read the restaurant reviews.

Maybe romance for its own sake is being revived. Last week, a young sportswriter said he wanted to take his new wife to *My One and Only*. "Yeah, I'm a sucker for that stuff," he said, sheepishly.

Ms. Lara supposes things are better now, without the old romantic delusions, but confesses, "I miss the madness, the muddle, the mystery. I want him to bring me tiger lilies he searched the creek bed for—even if what I really need is a new motor for the dishwasher." When you figure it out, do let us know, but hurry. These tiger lilies are wilting.

I too suspect things are improving. Romantics are slowly starting to come out of hiding, like woodchucks, peeking around to make sure it's safe. If marriage is back, can romance be far behind?

THAT IMPERFECT SOMEONE

I RAN INTO A longtime friend, Mort, who now runs a video dating service called Fatal Attractions, which matches people who are totally wrong for each other.

Mort says, "The more unsuitable someone is, the hotter they are. It's a new concept. If someone is too nice, our clients aren't interested. We like people with a prison record or a drug problem. They're irresistible."

He said, "The people we sign up are risk-takers. Many of our clients don't play tennis, jog or work out. Chasing unattainable people is the only exercise they get. Increases the heartbeat."

He added, "You're just in time for our June Princess Special on women who won't give you the time of day. They've got it all—brains, beauty, ego. You wouldn't stand a chance normally. We make it happen." My eyes lit up, but first I asked Mort how he began Fatal Attractions.

"I'd been to all the usual dating services and couldn't find the girl of my dreams," he said. "Nice but dull. I realized that the woman I *really* longed for were all wrong for me, yet I wanted just one date with them, for the hell of it."

"That's some success story," I said.

"We're onto something," he smiled. "We have more applications for Fatal Attractions than I can handle. People are lined up around the block for a chance to date a totally wrong person they won't ever forget."

"Are these mostly singles who have given up on meeting people through the usual video-dating channels?"

"They're burned out, many of them, sick of routine dates with decent people who are *also* wrong. They figure that, since they can't find the right person anyway, why not go for the gusto—major despair. Our motto is, More *angst* for the buck."

Mort slipped a cassette into the VCR to show me a a cross-section of his female clientele. A buxom bimbo appeared on the screen. "This is Marla," he said. "She's major trouble. Every guy wants her. She gives men the runaround, spends their money, makes impossible demands, won't call back and leaves you out in the cold."

"Hey, I see what you mean," I said. "She's terrific! I think I'm in love. How about her number?"

"Not a chance," said Mort. "Marla's booked up through New Year's Eve. But cast a gander at Tammi here. Talk about wacko. Tammi doesn't work, lives in a pig sty and reads nothing except menus, but men love the way she walks all over them."

"Don't these vixens take up time and energy?"

"Sure, but it's fun while it lasts," said Mort. "The trouble with meeting Miss Right is, you're tempted to settle down. At Fatal Attractions, we can guarantee that nothing serious will occur or triple your money back." He showed me a bulging folder full of angry, bitter letters from satisfied customers.

"What a novel way to avoid commitment," I said.

"Yep," he smiled. "We're about to franchise. By 1991, we'll have Fatal Attractions offices all over the map. We hope to become the Mrs. Fields of woe."

"Can you keep coming up up with losing matches?"

"We do 82 percent repeat business. Single people are tired of going out with the wrong person in a haphazard manner. Our clients are busy. Many travel. If you sign up and go to Chicago, say, just call our office and, within hours, we'll find someone to ruin your life."

"Have you anything in a wild woman who drinks, tells dirty jokes, listens to heavy metal, talks about her divorces and yet drives men mad with desire?"

"Be more specific. What color hair? Something in flaming red, perhaps, with a nice zany punk look?"

"Well, I'd prefer a blonde floozy in a miniskirt who watches game shows and sleeps all day."

"Meet Monique," he said, slipping in a cassette. "She's a former Miss Cigarillo. She'll make you suffer and beg for more. To know Monique is to loathe her."

"Sign me up," I said. "I've been trying to avoid someone like this all my life."

"You came to the right place," said Mort, rubbing his hands.

A NIGHT OUT WITH AN OLD STEADY

I F ALL ELSE FAILS, or simply palls, I take myself to dinner. I am, if I do say so, a fun date. Always on time; easily satisfied with even the most humdrum fare; and, to be sure, a constant source of amusement.

You might even say I'm one of my most reliable dates. After a few evenings in the company of other, decidedly more dazzling, personalities, I need a night off the town. Not a quiet night at home, catching up on ancient New Yorkers, which is a different sort of evening and fun in its own humble, slipshod way.

I refer, rather, to an intimate dinner with good old adorable me. Certain decisions must be made. Where shall we go? What shall I wear? Are work duds OK or should I go home first, freshen up and slip into something dowdier? No need to shave but, to pep myself up, I may don a snappier shirt and re-part my hair.

One never knows, after all, whom one might bump into. There's always that chance of being asked to share a table with a dark adorable stranger. This never happens, of course, since I am philosophically opposed to sharing tables, but one wants to look sharp.

My companion is a new issue of Spy. There are people capable of eating and staring into space with no printed matter before them. I find this not only impossible but vaguely sinful. I've done the bulk of my serious reading over chicken tostadas and Swissburgers.

I don't treat myself lavishly. A man of simple, if not shoddy, tastes, I can't bring myself to reserve a table for one at Chez Panisse. Not that I don't deserve it. It just would depress me.

There's also an ugly prejudice against anyone with the effrontery to dine alone. We are not welcomed with the open arms of parties of two. Indeed, a single person eating out is viewed as a sort of bum, a freak, an outsider—in brief, somebody taking up an entire table who will dawdle over coffee and leave half a tip.

When a host says, "Just the *one*, Sir?," I detect a note of pique tinged with pity, as he leads me directly to my usual table by the

men's room, the kitchen, the busboy's area or, if he's feeling especially vile, next to a party of 10 couples chatting merrily away, as if to say: "Single, eh? OK, pal, see how you like *this*."

I'm tempted to explain, "Yes, my good fellow, just the one—but then, you see, I am alone by choice and quite capable of rustling up a companion if I cared to."

Single people eating alone are shoved into dark corners so we won't ruin couples' appetites. In some restaurants we are asked to share a table, which goes against the grain of every self-respecting single. If we wanted to share a table, we'd get married.

No, we say politely but firmly, we do not wish to share a table. We wish to dine *à la carte*, thank you, provoking cruel punishment: banishment to the counter.

Here, amongst our fellow wretches, we are allowed to dine alone, as at a trough, elbow to elbow with other creatures not good enough to warrant an actual table with linen, flowers, little tent cards and, of course, a true waiter. Counter waiters, I sense, are either trainees or fill-ins or simply not good enough to wait on tables. We're also not allowed into booths reserved for "two or more." One is an odd, scrawny, naked number; not quite enough.

I always decline a counter and, much to everyone's annoyance behind me, explain that I will wait for a real table. Counters can be cute, in emergencies, but they do emphasize one's solitude, have a decidedly inferior feel and do not lend themselves to leisurely dining.

Some counters are cozy and peppy, but all counters are updated stockades. The knees are locked in place, a seat wobbles beneath and your eating arc is reduced, for fear of splashing your minestrone. Worse, there's no reading area, unless you've spent time on subways and can fold a newspaper into a napkin.

Solo diners are considered lonely guys, when they may well be having a better time than anyone (or any two) in the room. Other advantages of dining a cappella: No dull silences or the need for social niceties.

You may gaze about, gawk at women, yawn, nod off or concoct stories about the couples nearby, poor souls, striving so hard to have as much fun as you, with your new issue of Spy and the pleasant chatter of your own thoughts. OK, so it's not the Beaux Arts Ball, but a good time is had by one and all.

NO-FAULT DATING

I T'S TIME WE got the flab out of dating.

What people most dislike about singlehood is that it involves large amounts of pointless babble, double-talk, false enthusiasm and, basically, acting very little like your basic nifty self.

All this wasted energy exhausts people and makes them extremely vulnerable to such alternatives as nunneries, monasteries, even marriage. Dating is not efficient or cost-effective.

Thus, I am proposing a radically new approach to going out—Date-Enders.

Date-Enders is based on the truth-in-advertising and truth-in-lending concepts, to make dating easier, more open and honest, less time-consuming and, most of all, less jittery.

Date-Enders works like this: You call someone up for a date and ask her/him out, but before you even dial the number you ask yourself a series of questions, such as:

Do you *truly* want to spend an evening with this person? What are your motives? Are you going out because you want to, because your friends think you should, or because you like the body in question? Would you rather be at home with Robin Leach?

Once you've answered these questions to your satisfaction, you call the person up and ask said person out. You first preface it, however, by saying: "If you would prefer not to go out, simply say so. I can handle it."

If the person insists she would love to share a chocolate mousse, a date is set, after which you say: "I'll call the day before to see if you still want to do this or whether you've thought better of the whole idea."

This is based on the MacKenzie Rule, named for an old friend who first espoused a rule I employ when asked to do something I'm chary of—i.e., serve as a celebrity judge for a snake race, be a keynote speaker, appear on a panel or get auctioned off at a bachelor's ball.

The MacKenzie Rule states: "Whenever you're asked to take part in anything, pretend it's happening tomorrow. You'll always say no." This is based on the notion that anything sounds good a month from now.

When you're asked out, the normal feeling is to be flattered, which is where Nachman's Axiom comes into play: "The best thing about a cocktail party is being invited to it." This often applies to dates.

When you ask someone out, they're flattered. They then hang up and start thinking more clearly and wish they'd said no. Date-Enders sounds hardheaded, but it can cut down on those drab evenings you could avoid if you'd only been candid right away.

About here, someone is sure to say that unless one takes chances, one could miss out on some great times and meaningful relationships. This is remotely possible, so Date-Enders has come up with a useful self-help plan that allows for that rare splendid date.

It lets you take a chance on a date you're not sure about (most of them) and still bail out early. This self-destruct mechanism gives either person the opportunity to end the evening as soon as he or she is bored silly.

Since both members of Date-Enders have agreed to the ground rules, it's not awkward or painful. In time, this will become part of the normal going-out process. At Date-Enders, it only takes one party to cancel a date and it may be done up to five seconds before the date commences. Anybody can break a date, no questions asked.

Actually, this is a refinement of an earlier notion of mine, "the no-fault affair." With the no-fault broken date, either party may say, "I'd like to go home now" without giving a reason or being thought a weasel. This would avoid on-site prevarications—"I'm catching a 6 A.M. plane," "My gout is acting up again"—and allow you to get home in time to catch *Nightline*.

Assuming the date goes through as planned, all the way to the end, Date-Enders would prove itself more than worthwhile at the most crucial juncture of all—the front door. Date-Ender women would be allowed to jump out of the car and go inside without feeling an obligation to ask a man in; Date-Ender men could feel free not to make a pass without feeling unmanly.

Date-Enders would even allow dates to cut the other person off in mid-story (as in real life) by saying, "You told me this story already," "Can I talk now?" or "Who cares about *Phantom of the Opera*?" (or the Knicks/Nicaragua/your roommate's cat).

If you wish to break the dating habit completely, you may enroll in Date-Enders' six-week program, where you're gradually taken off candelit dinners and George Lucas movies. The plan involves aversion shock therapy, where men are shown photos of beautiful women accompanied by jolts of conversation about windsurfing, Harrison Ford and chlamydia.

BETTY AND/OR VERONICA?

I WAS REREADING "Archie" the other day, one of the major influences on my youth, possibly life.

I bought a copy of *Archie's Pals 'n' Gals* at Waldenbooks (they carry the entire Archie *oeuvre*) to see what the old gang was up to nowadays. It has been a while, but it looks the same, aside from some punk paper dolls, a VCR mention and a black guy; no sign of condoms.

Now, however, there's an entire comic book devoted to Betty and Veronica, a luxury we never had when I was a boy, but that was long before the women's movement.

The only woman with her own comic book then was Little Lulu, an early feminist—unless you count Nancy (a poor man's Lulu) and Wonder Woman (lovely, but trouble).

Betty and Veronica—and, to a lesser extent, Archie and his pals, Jughead and Reggie—occupy a special place in the psyche of men of a certain age for whom these two women were the first desirable *and* permissible female fantasies.

It was nasty to ogle Vargas girls in Esquire, but it was OK to have designs on Betty and Veronica, who seemed sexier than Vargas girls because they were virginal and, of course, unaware of what their male readers had in mind.

Rereading Betty and Veronica today, I see what a shrewd concept they are, the embodiment of all male fantasy, dilemma and folly: Two women, one Good and one Bad, who in fact are identical.

Even at 12, I realized that Betty and Veronica were the same girl. I wondered whether the artist could only draw one kind of face. Betty has a blond ponytail and is perky while Veronica is her twin except for long black satiny hair, a rich daddy and scheming ways.

Veronica is the Slut, Betty the Madonna, the one you were expected to admire. They had exactly the same figure, with just a hint of breasts—nothing lewd, but enough to get you thinking, although on Veronica it looked faintly seductive.

Archie liked them both, but he liked Veronica a little more even though she treated him badly. She was mean, indifferent, selfish, flirted outrageously and was only after Archie to prove her superiority over Betty, who bravely carried on. Betty was a good egg; eventually, of course, we knew Archie would marry her, but only if Veronica had a date.

Betty was cute but dull; Veronica was shrewd. Archie couldn't decide who he liked best so he dated them both. I was vaguely curious how this unlikely arrangement could exist, such a peppy *ménage à trois*.

Everyone got along, despite Veronica's scheming and Archie's indecisiveness. Betty and Veronica were best friends while "Ronnie" plotted. Betty calls her "my competition" with a sweet shrug.

In one strip, she muses, "You ask what I have to compete against her? My friends say I have a few other things going for me. They say I'm good-natured and have a sense of humor." Jughead pipes up, " . . . And you also make the yummiest chocolate chip cookies in town!"

Veronica may have fancy clothes and a rec room with a popcorn machine and video arcade, but Betty can cook. We know those cookies will triumph over evil.

"How does a simple girl like me compete against those tremendous odds?" asks Betty. In the last panel, we see her necking with Archie, and she winks: "I do it with old-fashioned persistency!"

So Betty has cookies *and* sex appeal, but it's not convincing. Can Betty's chaste kisses rival Veronica's lechery? Will Archie ultimately choose the lady or the tiger? Never. He has the best of each.

Ever the male (i.e., jerk), Archie still hasn't the slightest idea what's happening. He thinks they both like him when it's really a battle between the forces of blonde and brunette.

Archie isn't so much fickle as eclectic, and just nice enough not to crush the ever-resilient Betty. He says, "Knowing Ronnie, I've come to appreciate Betty even more." He has two tickets to a "Bruce Springsong" concert and, in front of Betty, asks Veronica to go. She agrees, haughtily, and the two gals go off together.

"Girls certainly are strange," says Archie. "They're not the least hit rational or logical like us boys."

Despite social/sexual revolutions, nothing has changed in Riverdale except that, now, everyone looks 14. I still like Betty. When I don't like Veronica.

SUNDAY IN THE DARK WITH ME

A FTER MANY MONTHS of Sundays (572 by actual count), I am still not sure what to do about them.

They just sort of lay there, like me, waiting for Monday. Even worse than Sundays are man-made Monday "holidays," which pass like a month in solitary. I will do anything to avoid a three-day holiday—in extreme cases, even go somewhere.

Nothing is more solitary than Sunday afternoon at 3 o'clock, a moment of truth for the unattached, when you know it's just you and your shadow. Not a sound in the house but a rustle of newspapers, maybe a faraway dog barking or the whine of a buzzsaw next door.

How you get from 3 P.M. to *60 Minutes* pretty much determines how content you are alone. Does the word "alone" itself give you shakes? Do you look up from the paper a lot? Are you talking to yourself and is yourself replying? Do you eat brunch as late as possible? Will dinner never arrive? Do you walk around the living room, peer through the blinds, take 4:30 tea breaks and keep checking the TV log to make sure you're not missing a great movie on Channel 44? Is it time to get cable? Do you hear phantom doorbells?

Actually, I only need to make it to *Inside Washington* at 6 o'clock, neatly segueing into *At the Movies* at 6:30, so it might be worse. Without *60 Minutes*, many more of us would be married by now.

Sunday at 3 P.M. can be a dark night of the soul, every bit as terrible as Fitzgerald's description of 3 A.M. For others, it's a sunny land full of evergreen possibilities—barbecues, lawn-watering, tanning, tennis, swimming, gardening, car washing.

Some weeks, I love Sundays; other times I hate them. Whatever mood I'm in, Sunday doubles it. I don't even mind a quiet Saturday night at home but a desolate Sunday can produce a Bessie Smith-size funk.

I've never liked Sundays, which I still associate with Sunday-school classes and dreaded childhood chores—cleaning garages, raking leaves. By comparison, school the next day seemed a picnic. (If my father were still around he would never tolerate my garage.)

When you're married, Sundays are full of critical tasks, which, if you're single, may be delayed until later, my favorite hour. A major up side of singledom is dragging out the garbage can just as the truck pulls up.

This is part of the vaunted "freedom" singles hear bandied about so much. "Freedom" doesn't only mean weekend orgies; much more often, it means having Sundays all to yourself, whether or not you want them.

If Saturday is for singles, Sunday is family day. On Saturday, the world is still open for errands, but Sunday is couple time: church, dinner with the kids, picnics, drives in the country, that sort of thing. When you're single, Sunday requires careful structuring. It should not be left to chance or, sooner or later, it'll get you down. Chart your day, hour by hour.

If you sleep late, you're in luck. There is nothing drearier than popping out of bed at 7 A.M. on Sunday, only to view a vast expanse of morning and afternoon stretching ahead of you.

If sleeping in won't work, quickly turn on *Sunday Morning*, a fine show and terribly underrated, hosted by Charles Kuralt, who seems sort of a lonely guy but jolly company.

I can get fairly forlorn if I think too long about the fact that I am actually watching TV at 8:30 Sunday morning when other people presumably are dressing for church or packing up the car for a trip to the lake. I'm not big on weekend trips, but I do enjoy the packing-lunch part.

Garage sales have gone a long way toward killing Sundays, or at least breaking its kneecaps. You may even meet someone at a garage sale; the little ladies who run them are always glad to talk and trade recipes. The trick, however, is not to let yourself get too morose poking through rusty waffle irons and wicker chairs that nobody wants anymore. Old ashtrays from Lake Tahoe can be pretty dispiriting.

By all means, do not sit around in a robe and slippers on Sunday, unless you want to induce terminal depression. The moment I change from slippers to shoes, I feel like a responsible citizen again. Shaving can also cheer you up, until you realize you're not going anywhere.

GIFT IDEAS FOR YOUR SEMI-LOVED ONES

THE LONGER YOU'RE single, the longer and more complex your Christmas list, as the branches of the extended family tree grow more gnarled and snarled.

What, after all, do you give a former involvee with whom you have exchanged every known intimacy? Just how intimate can you be? As you grope through the aisles, every gift idea drips with irony, symbolic overtones or plain old bad taste. Nothing seems right.

What do you give somebody whom you met only a month ago and are madly in love with who does not yet suspect your deepest desires? How do you find a gift for those people you See occasionally but are not Interested in? And how do you convey fond if not devoted feelings to someone who is more Interested in you than you are in them?

Christmas is a veritable minefield for the unmarried, whose relationships are always being tested for soft spots, pitfalls and wolf traps. Nothing like a major holiday to put things into focus.

Christmas is much easier when you're married and everybody is an official Loved One. You needn't measure your feelings with such hairline precision, as you do with a liked one, to be sure there are no hidden meanings in that soap dish. The most innocent gift on the surface may hold all sorts of secret significance—a lap robe, say, or towels or a welcome mat.

Should you buy a liked one something too nice, or not nice enough, it may be misunderstood, a problem every single person works long hours to avoid. A picture frame, for instance, is not a wise idea; a hope chest or crib is likely to be misconstrued.

Jewelry is a red-hot danger area, best avoided if any vagaries exist. Jewelry of almost any kind has serious undertones, as vases and coffee mills do not, and certain pieces of jewelry are more serious than others.

Pins, brooches and earrings are fairly innocent, assuming no precious metals or gems are involved. Bracelets and necklaces have romantic overtones. Rings of even the basest metal are to be given with utmost caution. A ring of any kind can have severe repercussions; this includes even a plastic Cracker Jack ring or cigar band.

You can't ever be sure what goes into a gift. I used to know a man who once bought two identical gold necklaces at Tiffany's as Christmas gifts, one for his wife and one for his mistress. Each of course, was delighted by such a personal, heartfelt expression.

Basically, anything that touches the skin is serious business, thus even a quilt or bubble bath may be treading on dangerous ground. Any item for the bedroom or bathroom is fraught with meaning, although I suppose a shower curtain would be all right— provided it's a *funny* shower curtain.

Anything humorous is fail-safe, which in itself may be a message you might not care to send, one that says that you consider the relationship frivolous, possibly even hilarious.

The best thing to get those female liked ones on your list is some form of fuzzy animal, which is playful, childlike and innocent; let her make of it what she will. A stuffed bear is still a classic crowd-pleaser. Not a mechanical teddy bear but a cuddly one to take to bed; perhaps a lifesize, inflatable bear.

Toys are the best idea, provided they're not "adult toys." One year, I got a wonderful little windup locomotive on a spiral racetrack—that's the sort of thing you want, something totally useless but endearing that makes you feel 12 again.

Wearing apparel is personal but impossible, entailing, as it does, choosing fabrics and learning sizes—calling up mutual friends and asking for people's bust measurements. A purse is nice (one size fits all) but I have purchased purses that were met with a look of dismay—something about the clasp being hard to open.

A purse, like gloves and scarves, is in the category of gifts that seem intimate but aren't. A calendar, likewise, is the perfect impersonal personal item for someone who has a thing for feminist poets or swimmers' buns.

A nice thing about living with someone is that you can confront them openly, which removes any surprise. One woman I know is giving her husband a bicycle pump and drill for Christmas; her main problem is whether he wants a quarter-inch or three-eighths-inch bit.

If the bedroom and bathroom are off-limits for single men, the kitchen is a safe area, maybe too safe. A salad spinner or trivet is not likely to come back and haunt you, but kitchen gifts are almost cold-bloodedly neutral—stuff you made for Mom when you were in Cubs.

Then, too, there's the age-old problem, dating back to the Wise Men, of whether to give anything at all. Should a red box unexpectedly be thrust into your hand on December 22, always keep a few cheese slicers in the trunk.

There are certain items that probably can't get you into any trouble—a car-cleaning machine, say, or a globe, or a nice cake plate, although these are really more for the mailman in your life.

FUNDAMENTALS
OF MINGLING

A WOMAN I KNOW says, "I wouldn't want to meet anyone I'd meet in a singles bar." *Not* a good attitude. If you want to be the darling of singles café society—and which of us does not—kindly wash away that sneer! Put on a happy face! Let a smile be your drink parasol!

Here are a few Hot Tips for Singles Bar Success:

Never Go Alone: Not even if your name is Warren Beatty or Nastassja Kinski. Even old Warren takes a friend along, or someone willing to pose as a friend, an expendable person you can ditch if you strike pay dirt. A *real* friend will not be annoyed that you (temporarily) prefer a total stranger to him or her.

If you're alone, people will assume you don't know anyone and are an untouchable. If you're with someone, it means at least one person can stand your company, even if it is someone of your own gender. If necessary, bring along a dull relative or a cardboard cutout of Joe Montana.

Move Mouth as if Talking: This is the main purpose of bringing a friend along. Standing alone silently invites pitiful looks and gives one a loner, if not nebbish, appearance. If you must go alone, pretend to be engaged in lively banter, with much laughing and tossing of the head.

Head-tossing is a vital component of female singles bar behavior, for it allows the woman to catch a glimpse of some guy over her shoulder while shaking out her hair, and also is a terrifically sexy gesture. Most women who do well at singles bars are expert hair-tossers. Do not, however, try to toss your hair if it's short.

Don't worry if nobody can hear what you're saying. Communication is not the point. If it's crowded, nobody will know the difference. If it's noisy, nobody will hear you anyway. The main thing is, get that mouth moving and keep it moving. Flash those teeth!

Don't Be Caught Gawking: Poor form. The main purpose of

talking is to give you a chance to make believe you're actively chatting when, in fact, you're sneaking little peeks at people over the shoulder of the person you're ostensibly addressing. This is a great social skill in single life, if not life in general—the ability to gaze directly at someone while staring at a point just beyond them, much like Dan Rather and Johnny Carson.

Say Cheese: Smiling is easier said than done. At single bars, an opening smile is more critical than an opening line. Be sure the correct person is looking at you when you smile, so you don't wind up charming the wrong person. Be sure they know you're smiling at them. Commit to a full smile. A half-smile looks like you're smashed or a little crazy. A crooked smile is good only in a punk crowd, where snarling is considered a turn-on. Practice that winning smile at home or in the rear-view mirror on the way over. Maintain a full repertoire of smiles—friendly, forlorn, mysterious, happy-go-lucky, boyish, roguish.

Learn How to Lean: Ordinary standing is boring and, after a few drinks, you may begin listing or be buffeted about by waitresses and people on their way somewhere. Leaning is cool. Get there early to find a decent leaning place. Forget the bar. A wall is good but has a wallflower aura. Go for the cigarette machine: You can set your drink on top and lean nonchalantly against it while supplying change to pert things buying Salems.

Circulate: It's always better to be in motion than not. Don't get wedged in a corner for two hours. Keep moving to give an impression of life, as if you've got people to see and places to go. This requires good elbow action and an ability to move in a sideways crablike motion. Think of it as slow-motion jogging. See how many laps you can do before leaving.

Look Adorable, Fascinating or Rich: If you're a man, you have your work cut out for you. A woman only has to look interesting, but a man must (a) look interesting *and* (b) pry a woman out of her corner and then out of herself, sometimes known as getting through to a woman.

If you're a woman, and many of you are, this means not sitting at a table with six people, of whom two or more are male. You female people who surround yourself with guys just are not playing fair. If you've got guys, why take up valuable space? Stop flaunting it. If you're single, act single, and kindly hold your harems elsewhere.

PHONEMANSHIP

I WILL GRANT YOU that the answering machine has its place. I dislike them generically, because they're machines. I'm still not quite at home even with a telephone, let alone my assistant telephone.

They may be a convenience, but is this convenience worth the trauma they put me through? Autophones are more than trendy appliances. They've taken over as a kind of grim butler who meets you at the door to announce, "Madame is not in, Sir."

Not "in," or just not in to you, pal? One never knows if the person is in or simply not taking calls at the moment. Unscrupulous types use a machine to screen calls. If they like the sound of the caller, they're home—a new form of one-upmanship. A subtle status is conferred when a friend picks up the phone in the middle of a recording and says, "Oh, hi, I'm actually here."

There's always a nagging suspicion when you get a recording that the person is indeed home but otherwise engaged—with a close friend, let us say, listening to you stutter away while they giggle, let us say, in bed.

Recently I spent a week trying to catch up to someone who had an answering machine. I wasn't trying to sell her anything. I was trying to ask her out. Three times I left the usual calling card data—time of call, day and night numbers, next of kin, etc.

A day passed, two days. I called again. No response. I tried a third time. Same thing, the old electronic brushoff. On my final try, a real person answered, full of apologies that she couldn't reach me. This is phone machine guilt, instilled by people who give up in disgust if your phone simply rings.

Swallowing hard, I made a date, gnashing my teeth all the while. A week later, I called to confirm and went through a fifth round of telephone tag. By the time we went out, I expected a robot.

If you leave a name and nobody calls back, insecurity sets in—no, paranoia. Possibly they never want to see you. I now employ an open-ended, future indefinitive reply: "If you care to call back, the number is . . . "

It is equally unsettling to own a machine and come home each day to no calls, just a grim, unblinking red light.

With a machine, people can't claim they weren't home, because, in a sense, they were home, or at least their ears were. If you need to cancel, it's nice to find just a machine home. And if you call at 11 A.M., you're *sure* to get a machine, which always takes bad news so beautifully.

If I'm home, I answer even at uncivilized times. People today feel free to call at all hours. When I first broke into telephoning, there was a gentleman's agreement that one never called after 11 or before 8 unless somebody was dead or in love. This was international law, governed by the Geneva Accords.

With the general collapse of society, people began calling at any old time, figuring that if you're asleep or not receiving calls, your machine would get it. Nobody's home anymore, or they pretend not to be. There's a hidden subtext on many machines: I'm out—why aren't you? I suspect people devise excuses to be out so they can switch on their alter ego.

I am rarely amused by answering service shtick. I prefer as little show biz as possible. Nothing like sitting through a bit you've already heard 20 times and are not real fond of, such as a tap solo or a Bach prelude or barking dogs. I was once so depressed by the jokes on a woman's machine that I didn't call back. Something about these answering machines brings out the lounge comic in otherwise normal people.

At the other extreme is the minimalist school, also the security-minded, suspicious characters who answer your happy "Hi!" with a somber, "You have reached 555-4053 . . ." It's like talking to a safe deposit box.

People who play music on their machine never quite get the sound level right. Their voice gets lost in an elaborate Quincy

Jones arrangement, or they have a lot of clever sound effects and so much production that I have no idea who's talking. By now, the fire department probably has a recording of "Too Darn Hot."

BEDTIME STORIES

LBERT HAD A crush on Ginny, a beautiful doctor. After months of trying, he finally got a date. Much to his delight and amazement, things quickly grew cozy. Indeed, after a few minutes on his couch, Ginny said, "You want to do it here or in your room?"

Still reeling from his good fortune, Albert said, "Here would be excellent."

"There's just one thing I have to tell you," she said. "I do live with someone."

"That doesn't bother me," said Albert, suddenly feeling very hip.

"You don't understand. My lover's a woman."

"I see," said Albert, trying to act as if he regularly dated lesbians. "And here I thought it was my irresistible animal magnetism!" He half-joked, "You still remember how?"

She did. He found Ginny passionate and uninhibited; it excited him. The next morning, he finally asked her why she wanted to sleep with him.

"Oh, I had an argument with my roommate. This is for spite. But I'd love you to meet Dana. She's great. You'll like her. Look, can you come over for breakfast?"

"I doubt if she wants to meet me."

"Don't be silly. You're no threat. It's like I went to a movie or something."

"Oh," said Albert. He took Ginny home. When she walked in, she got a big hug from Dana, whom Albert described later as "a very butch Chicana." As Albert watched, the women kissed and made up, after which the three sat down and ate Sunday breakfast together, then Albert left and Dana and Ginny lived happily ever after.

It was Darryl and Joan's first date and, after a romantic dinner and some rudimentary sofa play, Darryl suavely suggested they repair to the bedroom. "I can't stay here," she said. "My kids don't like me being out all night." Her kids were Davy, 9, and Gail, 13.

"So what now?" Darryl said.

"Come home with me," Joan said.

"Not yet," he said. "I've never met your kids."

"You can leave early if it bothers you. There's no need to worry, really." He reluctantly agreed.

The next morning, which arrived much too early, Darryl awoke at 7 to the sound of TV cartoons in the kitchen. Joan was asleep. He wanted to escape, but the only route was past the kitchen. Trapped!

Half an hour later, there was a knock on the door. "Mom, I'm cold. Can I come in your bed for a while?"

"Wait a second, Davy." Joan got up, went in the hall and Darryl heard feverish whispers. She came back to bed. "It's OK. Davy understands. Would you mind if he snuggled with me until he warms up?"

"Have you no shame, woman?" Darryl said. "Let me get dressed first. I should leave."

"Don't worry," kidded Joan. "Davy's very sophisticated about overnight guests."

"Yeah, but I'm not used to morning mystery guests. Is this a regular weekend ritual?" Davy hopped in bed next to his mother as Darryl fled to the other side and tried to look like a pillow.

"Hi!" said Davy, "Mom said you're a friend of hers." He put out his little mitt to shake.

"Your Mom and I are real old pals. I lost my house key last night, so your mother very kindly—"

"It's OK. Davy knows grownups sometimes sleep together even when they're not mommy and daddy."

"Everyone knows *that*," said Davy, turning to Darryl. "Hey, Daniel, you wanna see my new stamp?"

"Later maybe—and it's Darryl."

"What's going on in there?" said Gail, poking her head in the doorway. "Can I come in, too?"

"Really, Joan, I need to get home," Darryl said, nude under the covers, unable to make a move.

"Hey, don't go yet" said Gail. "I fixed breakfast for everyone. Smell?"

"Bacon," said Darryl. "No fair."

"Hi, I'm Gail!"

"I'm Darryl," he said. They nodded.

"I know," said Gail. "Mom told us you'd probably be staying over. I already set your place."

"Look, you never know," Joan said stifling a smile.

"Some do," said Darryl.

HAPPY HOUR FOR REFINED SINGLES

THE REASON MOST people keep away from singles bars is that, as everyone agrees, the conversation is empty and stultifying and the people are either dull or creepy.

What is needed, clearly, is a spa for the clever and cultured single, where only subjects of significance are discussed, but until such a place is built we may only imagine what it might be like.

As you enter our fantasy saloon, your ID is checked at the door. "Hold on, fella," says a small bespectacled man with a beard. "This sheepskin says a B.A. in bus. ad. from Reno Polytechnic Institute. Afraid you'll have to leave. Sorry. Come back when you're more interesting."

When once inside, however, you are stunned by the calm, quiet atmosphere of the place. Overhead, the subdued music of Eric Satie plays. A TV set above the bar shows *Otello* with the sound off.

"I can't believe the arms on Domingo," whistles one regular to another over sherry. "Nobody can match him as the Moor. He's Verdi's main man."

An argument ensues over whether Domingo could have whipped Caruso in his prime. An elderly man, overhearing them, sets down an aperitif and says, "Aria for aria, Enrico was a lock. He had all the moves. Placido's top register is ragged. He oughtta hang it up."

Another man at the bar stops playing liar's chess and asks everyone, "Bet nobody here can tell me what Caruso sang when he first broke into La Scala!"

"I'm weak on opera trivia," says a dowager. "Try me on Renaissance sculpture or anything Chaucerian."

Down at the other end of the bar, two women are seated in booths, one perusing *Walden*, the other engrossed in a collection of John Stuart Mill essays. A man approaches them and says, "Hiya, ladies. Can I buy a round? What're you gals thinking tonight?"

One looks up and says, "Oh, my usual—Thoreau. Emerson makes me too drowsy and I have to drive home. Why?"

"No reason," he smiles. "I'm a Hawthorne man myself. I started reading Hawthorne in college and just never changed. I always dug those New England Transcendentalists." She smiles.

He pulls up an arm chair. "So—you girls read here often?"

"This is our first time at Sigmund's," says the other woman, closing her volumn. "We're meeting a poet friend later. Naturally, I'd *heard* of Sigmund's, in the New York Review of Books, but the whole singles literary scene is such a drag."

"I love their personals," he says. "I used to go with a woman I met through a New York Review ad, but it didn't last. She was too into semantics. All I wanted was an amateur linguist for a weekend seminar."

He asks, "Say, either of you ladies have a quarter change? I passed the jukebox on my way in, and there's a tune I just gotta play. Haven't heard it in years. Remember 'Greensleeves'?"

One of the women shouts, "I can't believe it! It's *only* my all-time favorite Elizabethan folk ballad, that's all! Who do they have doing it?"

"The Roger Wagner Chorale," he says. "They've got a great sound."

She rolls her eyes, "Hey, wow, tell me about it. I've got all his albums. The new one is really hot. Their Handel beats anything I've seen on Mormon Tabernacle video."

He frowns, "Yeah, the Tabs haven't sung anything decent in years. When they tried to cross over, they lost me. I can't listen to their 'Messiah' anymore."

"Ya know, this isn't bad for a singles reading room," remarks one of the women, looking around.

"I generally drop by on my way home from the office to unwind with The Economist," he says. "By the way, I've got an extra ticket to the Joffrey next week, if one of you gals is free. They're doing 'The Firebird.'"

One woman grins, "Jeez, I'd love to go—I'm like a *real* Stravinsky freak—but we just met and . . ."

"Hey, no problem," he says. "We'll have a drink first and then decide. You got a business card on you?"

She fishes in her PBS tote bag and pulls out a card. "You can call me at the museum anytime. I'm always there. Just ask for Dee in the Cro-Magnon wing."

COOKING FOR IDIOTS

I HAVE THE MAKINGS of a good husband in at least one crucial area: groceries. I'm one heck of a shopper, if I say so myself. I love the entire ritual, from the bumpercarts to the bagging and check-cashing ceremony.

Supermarkets are a source of endless fascination and amusement. Those endless rows of cookies and cheeses make my eyes dance, each cereal representing years of patient research by General Mills as they try to breed a Cheerio with a Grape Nut.

One reason I am in such awe is that all this remains a vast alien country, cans stretching as far as the eye can see—jams for days, pickles everafter. I am like a Czech immigrant in this land of plenty. It seems overwhelming and awesome, well beyond my scope of experience. I do not know veal chops from pork loin. The world of muffin mixes and puddings is foreign to me. I do not speak the language; Uncle Ben, Betty Crocker, Duncan Hines and Aunt Penny are not my kin.

For decades, I have wheeled past shelves and bins wondering, what is this stuff? In one bin lay ears of corn. I have eaten corn; I have bought corn. But until last week I never truly contemplated corn until I decided to buy an ear, cook it and consume it.

This may seem a trivial exercise, yet for a man who has never thought deeply about corn, it loomed as a major culinary adventure. Is it possible, you ask, that a man can be my age and still be unfamiliar with this most basic of foods, so American and symbolic—waving stalks, etc.?

It is extremely possible. Until last week, I had never dealt with corn on a one-to-one basis. I felt myself ready, having mastered mashed potatoes six weeks earlier. I use the term "mastered" cavalierly. I triumphantly mashed them once, following precise instructions, but six weeks passed between mashings and I had to ask for brush-up lessons.

So I bought an ear of corn—two ears, in fact, feeling bold. Much to my surprise, the kernels began wrinkling the next day. It was my first lesson: corn does not sit idly by, like apples and carrots, waiting to be summoned. It ages. Time and tide and corn wait for no man.

I tried again, this time purchasing only one ear of corn, having been humbled. Buying corn for me involves mainly peeking inside the husk to see if there are indeed kernels of corn in there, as advertised. I bought it with some trepidation. All corn looks the same—ah, but is it?

That evening, I peeled off the husk and fine silk threads, all 2700 of them, afraid they might be poisonous. Somehow I knew that corn required boiling, but quickly questions began to gnaw at me: Should the water boil first? Is the pot covered or uncovered? When is corn "done"?

Stupid questions, but not to me. A woman friend suggested *The Joy of Cooking*. "Surely Irma Rombauer doesn't deal with something as dumb as how to boil corn," I said. (As it happens, bless her, she does.)

All on my own, I reasoned that corn must be in the mashed potato ball park and so I (a) brought the water to a boil, then (b) added salt—only to find the salt shaker empty and the corn too long for the pot. As my water boiled, I groped for a paring knife but it wouldn't saw corn. Thinking fast, I grabbed a butcher knife.

When you're a cooking moron, everything goes wrong. I poured salt into my salt shaker—itself a new experience—only to find it wasn't filling up. I looked down to see salt flowing through the holes onto the floor. (Culinary tip: When refilling salt shaker, plug up holes before turning over.)

A major crisis and the corn wasn't even in the pot yet. At such moments, I realize why I eat out. I put in a few pinches of salt (more guesswork), sawed the corn in two, dumped it into the bubbling water and gave it five minutes, unsure exactly how long you boil corn.

If you ask a real cook, she shrugs and says, "Oh, until it looks done." This means nothing to a cooking idiot. Someone else says it depends on how ripe the corn is. If it's tender, seven minutes; if mature, 10 minutes. What's tender? It looked mature yet tender—sort of early middle age.

To me, it looked like your basic ear of corn—quite a remarkable work. I hated to eat it. I studied the rows of yellow pearls, each as perfect as snowflakes, and marveled at the wonders of the universe. My eyes misted.

Pulling myself together, I noted the time and readied the butter. After six minutes, I saw kernels falling off in the water and decided this must be God's way of saying it's time to eat.

I fished out the corn, swabbed it in butter and, without further ado, gnawed away. Yum! Just like corn on the cob mother used to boil. I doubt if even Irma Rombauer could have improved on it. Now that I've got mashed potatoes and corn nicely in hand, I just may give broccoli a shot. Hell, you only go around once.

ARE YOU SWINGING OR DANGLING?

E VERY SO OFTEN, a single person comes face to face with a
gut issue: Am I swinging and, if so, how much?
This is an anxiety that couples rarely come up against.
While the term itself has been officially laughed out of existence,
any single person wants to think he's swinging just a *little*, or
what's the point of month-to-month rent?

Single people have a nagging suspicion that other people are
out there swinging without them. This is a myth, of course, pro-
mulgated largely by married people who live in fear that they're
missing something.

It's what I call the Other Party Syndrome, where you never feel
you're at the right party. Or, in this case, any party at all.

If you're scooping onion dip out of the carton at 8 P.M., chances
are pretty good you are not at a party and will not be swinging on
this particular evening.

When you're single, the so-called action often seems to be
where you're not, but you can't be sure, since nobody has devised
an accurate measure for swinging.

By answering the 17 questions below, you will be able to determine the arc of your swing. Only you have the correct answers,
of course, locked away in your heart.

1. When the phone rings, does it tend to be your mother? Do
you check your answering machine after you've been in the
shower?

2. When you come home after work, is the high point of the
evening going through the mail? Do you check out the pennies-off
coupon packet and open the Reader's Digest Sweepstakes with
trembling fingers?

3. Come Saturday night, do you ever think of calling up former
lovers to see if they're home, too?

4. When did you last change the sheets (not just the pillow cases)?

5. When you call for a third date, do you still have to identify yourself and state your place of employment?

6. Is your address book primarily filled with the names of people you haven't seen since 1974? Why aren't they crossed out yet?

7. Do you know the names of the characters on *The Cosby Show*?

8. In the last month, how many dates had to cancel because of friends coming in from Cleveland?

9. Do you find yourself flirting with waitresses/bus boys/grocery clerks more than usual?

10. How many times in the last six months have you gone through your old high school yearbook? Are you looking forward to the next reunion?

11. Have you been taking home a lot of work from the office, and actually getting it done?

12. When a Jehovah's Witness comes around to the door on weekends, do you engage him or her in lively conversation? Have you ever dated a Fuller Brush Man?

13. Are you seriously considering placing a singles ad? Taking a life-drawing class? Going on a Club Med cruise? Enrolling in a health club to meet people? Joining a church group?

14. On Sunday afternoon about 4:30, do you start fixing dinner?

15. Have you begun thinking about owning a pet? Are you buying more plants than is strictly necessary, just for company?

16. The last time you went to a single's hangout, did you find yourself making eyes at a cheeseburger in the back room a little sooner than you'd planned?

17. Is your Saturday night spoiled if it's another *People's Court* rerun?

DATE YOUR WAY
TO WISDOM

NOT EVERYONE SEES dating as fear and loathing, hell on earth or, as one date recently put it, "a highly unnatural way to get to know people."

Some people see it as a big adventure, full of mystery, comedy and juicy stories you can live on for months—plus a few crucial things I'd like to get into.

Sure, dating has its moments of agony and ennui, its pain and poignancy and slapstick comedy, but one reason it keeps drawing people back into the fray is the pull of the Great Unknown.

There you are, driving toward a strange new house in an obscure part of Berkeley, not knowing what lurks there—an evening of tedium? Intense talk? Approach/avoidance techniques? Fun and games? Maybe the Love of Your Life (the odds ought to increase with each date).

Rarely does the latter occur—no more than 10 times a year—but the contemplation of it, the merest glimmer of the possibility, is part of the evening's giddy overtures as the curtain rises on yet another night of heavy drama or wry banter.

If you go out, you must learn to savor the entire dating experience, the pre-dinner tension and post-goodby unease. Approach each date like a trip to an exotic untraveled land—Paraguay, say, or Lebanon. Anything can happen! Dating is twice as broadening as a week in Peru; also, you can drink the water and there's less chance of encountering bandits.

First of all, dating increases your knowledge of areas you formerly had no interest in—often, as it turns out, for a good reason. I don't mean obscure hamlets in the Santa Clara Valley; I mean areas of commerce and industry.

Without dating, I would be ignorant of Apple computer's hiring practices, the packaged-nuts business, how to open an art gallery, high school security measures, the real estate scene, TVcommer-

cial production, banking practices, writing ad copy, opening a PR business, librarianship, free-lance photography, quilt collecting, running a bed-and-breakfast and, most intriguing of all, what goes on behind the scenes in the teeming world of dental health insurance.

I've also learned an astonishing number of ways to prepare salmon, the fine points of California sauternes and how to tell a stale pear tart at a glance.

If I had done nothing on dates but pay attention to the food, I might be an accomplished chef by now, but I was not paying attention to the food. I was listening.

I have thus become proficient at pretending to listen to an excited waiter unreeling the day's specialties without once cracking a smile, no mean feat. Two years ago, I could barely stifle a giggle, so I have come a long way in this one area alone; it should stand me in good stead the rest of my non-dating life.

Because of dating, I've also become a crackerjack parallel parker. Before I was single, I couldn't maneuver a car into tight places or park on corners. I knew no secret alleys in Chinatown. I didn't know the difference between a green and a white zone. I was unable to find my way out of the park after dark. Happily, I am a changed man, and I owe it all to dating.

I have also become surprisingly adept at social survival techniques, the ability to find something fairly interesting to say during conversational lapses you could drive a truck through.

A few simple tricks can get you past serious lulls, such as inquiring into the number and sex of a date's siblings (13 minutes), comparing the Price Club to CostCo (7.5 minutes), and contrasting the cultural life of San Francisco with Los Angeles, New York or your date's prior place of residence (27 minutes).

Perhaps most impressive of all, dating has taught me how to shower, shave and dress in an hour. Four years ago, my best time was 96 minutes. Only two months ago, I drove home, showered, shaved and donned a tux in under one hour. I doubt if Fred Astaire could beat that, even in his prime.

RED INK

I S WRITING LOVE letters a lost art, like marriage? There was a time, not so many centuries ago, when it was a literary form. Nobody writes love letters like D. H. Lawrence or Anais Nin, whom one suspects were also pouring out their hearts for readers yet unborn.

Recently, I bought a remaindered copy of some classic love letters edited by Lady Antonia Fraser—an expert, I figured, and no doubt the recipient of some hot stuff from Harold Pinter: *"Dear Antonia! It seems . . . Yes! . . . There is a . . . romance! . . . But. No . . .*

These letters are closer to essays—written, no doubt, for the critics. They go on for hours. You wonder how Keats ever got any real writing done. Nobody writes love letters like those 20-pagers the Brownings used to crank out every morning.

People now prefer to pick up the phone, but a phone is inhibiting. The other surrogate form of love letter is the new, tasteful, $3 card embossed with sentiments by minor poets, silhouettes of swans and fold-out Monet waterlilies. A call or a card is not a love letter. You can't go over it 37 times, can't put it in a secret place and sneak little peeks, can't study the phrasing, penmanship and punctuation for hidden meanings.

A love letter is a major effort and mustn't be dashed off on yellow legal pads, typewriters or laser printers. No matter how impassioned, a printout hasn't the same romantic weight as flimsy lavender paper.

Ideally, a fountain pen is required, assuming one is proficient at graphology; your great letter writers will work only with a Mont Blanc. Lacking a talent for swirls, or $150, a fine-tipped Le Pen will do. Any love letter is better than none, but it takes an edge off things if a letter is filled with ink splatters and butter stains. Never write a love letter while eating toast.

You need moody pastel paper—not lined 3-hole paper, office stationery or a message pad from a Best Western Motel. Before starting, be sure to have enough inspiration to last more than half a page. A two-paragraph love letter lacks punch, signing off suddenly with, *"OK, soulflower, that about wraps it up from here."*

Try to drain your soul in one sitting. You'll never be able to rekindle the initial fire a week later and will need to rev yourself up, making you feel somehow shady. Better to send an unfinished love letter than a padded one: *"So as I was saying, my heart is filled to overflowing . . ."*

Love letters are best written late at night, but not so late that you're half asleep and incoherent, although a certain amount of babbling is expected, even endearing. Too much coherence makes one sound suspiciously in control of one's senses, suggesting that you knock these suckers out by the ream. You shouldn't sound too studied, as if you spent hours in Roget's looking up synonyms for "lips."

You must also make sure that your passion strikes just the proper tone and sounds real. Too much emotion seems labored; not enough, like consommé. It's best not to slip in too many quotes from Proust. It'll only make your own stuff sound banal and juvenile.

Don't write too many love letters the first few weeks or go on too long, for there *will* come a time when the letters start tapering off and you'll need to make a lot of lame excuses about your pen going dry.

Try to keep the letters under six pages, for new lovers are highly sensitive to the merest trace of a lessening in feeling and sure to worry that a shorter letter means you don't care as much anymore. Women count the words and can tell by the loops in your "g"s if it's all over. To ward off lover's paranoia, cut up those early 25-page jobs into sections and save them for a rainy day.

One problem with love letters is that they age badly and can become a storage problem. You want to keep them, naturally, if only because burning seems cruel—unless, of course, you despise your ex-heart's desire. In movies, people are always tossing old love letters into the fireplace, which has a nice theatrical flair, especially if your wife's around.

Reading old love letters can be unbearably torturous. As a friend who is back in love wrote me recently, upon going through carbons of his old letters to her: "It's so depressing to believe I've said the same things so many times to so many people—and totally believed it each time."

A few years ago, I found some old love letters written in college, later returned to me. By the second paragraph, I was a wreck. Equally sad is that my handwriting has not improved since I was 18.

Old love letters belong in shoe boxes, with pink bows around them, not because you plan to read them some day but just as a way of giving them a decent burial. There's no point in exhuming the charred remains of an old flame; however, it's nice to keep the ashes, even if the urn is just an old Hush Puppies box.

RENT-A-MATE

A T FIRST IT DIDN'T seem as if the idea had a chance, but Morty Mifflin now believes the time is ripe for surrogate husbands.

"Surrogate mates are the wave of the future," Mifflin noted this week in his office at Acme Spousal Support Systems, a husband brokerage he just opened in Sunnyvale.

"Maybe there's something to this social engineering, after all," I said. "I wouldn't have thought it possible for couples to be so rational about something so personal. Look what's befallen surrogate moms."

"Oh, tosh!" said Mifflin. "What's one lawsuit? They just need to iron out some of the wrinkles. Surrogate motherhood still has potential, but not like this service. It's simplicity itself. A man who believes he cannot be a natural husband, for whatever reason, hires us to provide a surrogate hubby to spend time with his wife."

He sat back in his chair. "To take an example: Let's say that on weekends, when the legal husband would rather be watching football, playing golf or poker, going fishing or just dozing on the couch. His wife feels neglected. She thinks he should be tending to household chores or taking her hiking."

Mifflin noted that screen-door fixing was in steep decline until he began providing surrogate husbands.

"Now, any wife who feels her natural husband is goofing off can sign up with us and we assign a man to go to her home on weekends or whenever and give the old man a rest."

His agency provides men for everything from taking kids to the movies to fixing candlelight dinners. I asked how natural husbands feel about all this.

"They love it more than their wives and are often the ones who suggest the idea in the first place. It takes a huge burden off them."

"Isn't there a danger that a surrogate husband and the wife who contracts for his services may become attracted to one another?"

"No chance," said Mifflin. "You see, they all sign a contract and that's that. The surrogate husband promises to go away when his work is done, the wife agrees not to fall in love with him and the real husband vows not to get jealous. Feelings don't play any part in it."

I said I didn't think that such a far-fetched plan would appeal to very many couples. He hooted, "Don't be such a fuddy-duddy!"

I asked Mifflin what else the surrogates do, and he smiled.

"You name it. OK, I know what you're thinking, but the answer is no. Most wives are eager to find a surrogate hubby so that her legal husband feels free to relax. She's not neglected, he feels no more guilt, they're attracted to each other again and I make a few bucks."

"Why don't you also provide surrogate wives?"

"Maybe down the road. We test-marketed it in Iowa, but not enough wives went for it."

He added, "It's still a viable concept, but the catch is that husbands have fewer demands. Mostly, they just want to be left alone, so there's nothing much for a surrogate wife to do, except maybe tell the husband he's just wonderful the way he is and not to bother himself about romantic dinners or new shelves and to watch all the football he likes."

"So you find couples are interested?"

"This has replaced counseling. The idea is to relieve marital tension. We guarantee 25 percent more domestic bliss or double your money back. Surrogate Spousal Support supplies the crucial missing bliss factor that causes so many rifts."

I asked what kind of men sign up to be surrogate husbands. "A lot of young studs, sleazy gigolos and would-be lotharios, I suppose."

"Not at all," he said. "Mostly, it's older husbands who just want to do a little moonlighting."

LITE DATING

L AST WEEK after six months, I caught up with my old ineligible bachelor friend, Guy Solo.

I asked what it was like these days out in the intrepid world of the unattached. Guy said that, rather than playing the field, he is now playing it safe.

"Did monogamy finally nail you or are you just in mourning for Hugh Hefner?" I inquired, as we met for a drink at the Cirque Room, a local doubles bar.

"Neither," he said. "I'm going out a lot, but with women friends."

"An interesting, indeed inventive, solution, and recommended by 9 out of 10 physicians."

"Oh, it's definitely healthier, but also much more fun than your regulation garden-variety date."

"By which you mean females with whom you might be romantically involved?"

"Precisely," said Guy. "I finally got fed up with the sexual tension of dating and, as a diversion, began asking out women

friends—ex-lovers, otherwise engaged women, office mates, etc. It's fabulous. I strongly advocate dating female friends. Could be the wave of the future."

"Indeed," I said. "I've secretly tried it myself and, while it struck me at first as a bit kinky, I've warmed to the idea. I thought people might talk, spreading rumors that I was either a monk, homosexual or a misogynist."

Guy nodded. "It's worth the risk. Female friends make great dates. Many more laughs. The whole evening is so relaxing you almost never want to see anyone else. The down side, of course, is that a friend offers everything but sex."

I shrugged. "To quote the late great Joe E. Brown, 'Nobody's perfect.' Just think of it as Lite Dating."

He remarked, "I'd never considered going out with non-lovers before, but since the sexual revolution there are all these wonderful ex-lovers floating around."

Guy said, "Why should gays have all the best female friends?"

"Excellent point. In fact, some of my best friends are women."

Guy smiled, "I never enjoyed ordinary dating the way I do close friends. I had no idea dating could be so much actual fun."

"What do you do with these women friends?"

"That's the best part of Lite Dating. You can do whatever you like, unlike heavy dating. No need to impress friends who already know all your flaws, no dumb game-playing or need to measure up, and no searching for signs."

I whispered, "Look, I wouldn't want this to get out but I'm currently dating three women fairly steadily myself—all close female friends."

"But you still go out with, you know, strangers?"

"Only if absolutely necessary," I confided. "Now and then, just to stay in practice, I'll take out someone I just met. I always have such a trying time that I come running back to my women friends to tell them about it."

"I love sharing horror stories," Guy laughed. "It's like post-mortem party trashing. They tell me about their terrible dates and, before you know it, we're having these intense, meaningful discussions and getting real close."

Guy wondered, "Why can't it be like that with non-friends?"

"I guess you have to go through all the banalities before you're allowed to act real."

"I'm worried, though," he said. "Lately, I find myself becoming attached to these friends."

"I know what you mean. Old girlfriends are a real turn-on. Just pray it doesn't start up again. Sex can be the end of a beautiful friendship."

HAVE YOURSELF A MARRIED LITTLE CHRISTMAS

THE FIRST THING A single person notices about married couples, once we get inside their houses, is how incredibly well-organized they are—at least on major holidays, at least on the surface. Even if it is just surface, I'm impressed; I'll settle for a calm, dust-free surface.

Possibly it's deceptive, but the place is humming; the house is in shape—a clean, well-lighted place where child-size organisms can grow. No swaying towers of old newspapers in the corner or stacks of mossy dishes. Aromas drift in from the kitchen. A fire blazes in the living room. Children and pets cavort on the carpet. All the plants are watered and thriving.

Such a welcoming place, married people's houses! They look so—well, lived in. A single person's house may be tidy, even pretty, but after visiting a married home, one's own house is like crawling back into a dank cave. Or so it seems when you visit; behind the scenes, it may well be a Chinese restaurant kitchen.

Even the most confirmed single person admires all this domestic efficiency, may begin to envy it and be duped into marrying in the hope of duplicating it. If nothing else, marriage (like Samuel Johnson's comment on hanging) tends to concentrate one's attention.

As a former Married Person, 3rd class, I realize it only seems this way when you're single and view domestic life as a tourist. When you're on the other side, you know that chaos lies only a closet away.

Most single people have no need to get their act together, as do married couples, who must organize to survive. If a light goes out in my kitchen, I can grope in the dark for days until summoning the wherewithal to change it. No such nonsense is allowed in married homes. Tasks get done or all life stops.

In the midst of all this jolly holiday commotion, a single guy feels odd and apart, a stranger in a strange land. Most days, he enjoys this tourist status, but on Christmas he feels on the defensive, on the outside peering in. Not quite sad, but his identity is in question.

Married people have got things under control. They know where all the pans are. They can find the fuse box, the whisk broom. All the clocks work. They have pianos. The hedges are trimmed. Their Raisin Bran isn't soggy. They own watering cans, irons, wrenches. They put out bowls of fruit and *linen*. The very word "linen" is never uttered by a single person until married, nor foreign terms like "spackle" and "grout."

Marrieds lay in supplies of ant killer and Baggies and aluminum foil. The garbage pail is always lined, the mouse traps set, the cookie jar filled. Whereas singles live by their wits, married people remain girded for action.

Single folks, except for the resourceful few, muddle through. Singles are self-supporting, mere drifters between November and January, yuletide flotsam and jetsam.

Most of us don't know what to do when things break, or whom to call. We wring our hands and weep silently, until, in desperation, we call mother or a married friend for the names of plumbers, maids and electricians.

Married people *know* all this stuff. They can put their hands on roofers and last year's W-2 forms; they have accordion files and insurance forms and, yes, wills! Single people assume either they're going to live forever or that nobody will know if they're gone.

It's rather weird to venture into darkest suburbia, the land of the married. A woman I know, after visiting a couple over Thanksgiving, reported how she was shaken by the quirks of her domestic friends. "We're talking mounted fish on the wall!" she gasped.

You'll rarely find a mounted fish on the wall of a single person. You will never find a copy of Sunset on a hall table. Chances are you won't even find a hall table, not with a vase of flowers on it. Married people (and certain rare, efficient unmarried females) are into flowers. Also corkboards, shelf liners, air fresheners, toothbrush holders and knife racks. I bought a knife rack, with every good intention of hanging it, but it's still in the drawer: if I were married this would be a scandal.

Christmas is tough on singles, and calls for all of our powers of survival. Though I revel in the good cheer, I try to view it as an annual promotional event for marriage.

While this can be a horrible time of year to be single, an idea spread by couples who feel mighty smug all snug in the bosom of their families, with a little cunning any veteran single can turn Christmas back into a pagan ritual—a month-long bacchanal of feasts, teas, eggnog parties and tree-trimming orgies.

Remember: *Being single means never having to cook Christmas dinner.* That's a major plus right there. Nobody expects you to provide more than a bottle of wine or, at most, a pumpkin pie.

With a little advance planning, you can be inundated with invitations from people who feel sorry for you. Never mention your own family. Keep them in the background. Play the orphan; work on those misty far-off gazes.

Let people think you have nowhere to go. Sulk a lot. Stare out windows and say things like, "Gee, this used to be my favorite time of the year, when Gram and Gramps were alive."

If married people are cruel enough not to insist that you come to their house for Christmas, merely mention how your whole family used to bundle into the sleigh and drive out to the farm on Christmas Eve, when you were a kid.

This is, of course, a teentsy lie but then this is a desperate time of year and desperate measures are called for. As a yuletide single, one must occasionally take the reindeer by the horns.

You can't sit around waiting for holiday invitations when you're single; there's always a fair chance that there won't be any. It's never too early to begin working on holiday guilt; I usually start in around Halloween.

What you do is, you go up to married people in the office and say, "Going home for Christmas?" If they say no—as they likely will—that's your clue to say, "Me, neither. I was thinking of going to Acapulco, just to get away—I always get too sad over the holidays."

If this draws a blank, you say, "Hey, did you read that the Hyatt has a *terrific* Christmas dinner deal? They've got a pastry cart and everything! Kiwi tarts just like granny use to make."

Should someone tentatively inquire into your holiday plans, you simply frown and say, "I haven't thought much about it, actually, I may go back home, if I can scare up the money. I'll probably just buy a turkey and drop it off at St. Anthony's dining room on my way in to work."

When the married person says, "You have to *work* on Christmas?," you respond with a bored shrug, "Oh, just to have something to do. I hate sitting around the house all day Christmas—it's so dreary."

Then you add (with downcast eyes), "Aw, I don't like turkey and cranberry sauce and candied yams and fresh popovers and piping hot mince pie all that much anyway. Chances are, I'll end up at McDonald's. *Ha ha!*"

Once you've got at least one Christmas dinner nailed down, you can then concentrate on finding time to be with your actual family, whom you've kept on hold as long as possible, for use as a last resort.

Your own family should, of course, take precedence, but there *is* a pragmatic side to be considered: The chances are not that great of meeting someone at grandma's house who's cute and single. Most mothers, I find, are understanding, if you explain that someone has invited you to a Christmas dinner that includes yummy single women with all the trimmings.

Also, after a few years of being single, you get out of the habit of making small talk with relatives and might end up asking Aunt Hannah what her sign is or if she's doing anything after dinner.

Ideally, you will want to put in a token appearance at home before hitting a friend's home where there just may be a single person on hand with whom to share a wishbone.

IS THIS RELATIONSHIP GOOD FOR YOU, TOO?

THERE IS A DREAD, widespread, little-discussed social disease that is virulent among singles, and I think we need to discuss it openly.

I speak of *relationshipiasis*, an inflammation of the inner couple that causes a burning sensation and great pain, not unlike—well, shingles. This psychic rash may be defined as the practice of discussing a relationship until it's ruined. One case I know involves a man who, 20 minutes after he met a woman he liked, began delving into the nature of their relationship. A week later, it was all over, talked into an early grave.

An early warning sign is an overuse of the word "relationship"—as in, "Where's this relationship heading?" Women are the major carriers. Some couples prefer talking about a relationship to having one; people who used to date now relate. You know a relationship is in trouble when all you do is discuss it.

There are now relationship classes, books, seminars—entire careers carved out by people speaking to folks about relationships and how to have one. People discuss relationships as if they were blenders: "It isn't working"; "It doesn't meet my needs"; "It's too messy."

What is this thing called relationship? (Other musical favorites include: "Our Relationship Is Here to Stay," "Relate to Me or Leave Me.") Women, always more acutely aware of the nature of relationships, and life generally, tend to bring it up first. Men, being men, tend not to know what the hell they're talking about. I heard of a woman who turned to a man in bed and asked, "Are we having a relationship?" Tests proved positive.

The malady often begins with a woman saying, "How do you see our relationship a year from now?" Right away, a man is baffled and mute. He didn't realize he was supposed to see it *any* way, let alone a year from now.

When a woman senses a relationship is "not going anywhere" (i.e., where she'd like it to go), chances are she'll bring it up. This startles the Old Male, who would rather tough it out than talk it out. The New Male can be prodded into throwing a relationship down on the floor and examining it, to show he's a good sport.

Men are known to leave home when pushed by women to discuss how they really feel about their relationship. A guy goes out for a pack of Winstons and never returns; it happens all the time. He ends up in a saloon, blubbering, "Gus, I loved that woman but I couldn't take another day of our goddamn relationship."

While men are content to let a relationship idle—the Nathan Detroit Syndrome—a woman will claim it's "stagnating." Women maintain mental graphs on which they chart relationships, like Dow-Jones averages—up 4 points on Monday, down 13 points by Friday's closing. If a woman detects a blip, she'll say, "Something's going on in our relationship we should talk about." This search for the elusive "it" can take months.

"It's so *seventies* to talk about relationships," moans one talked-out woman I know. "All that gestalt-Esalen stuff. A relationship is whatever it is; what's to talk about? It's the one thing I never bring up in a relationship. I'd much rather talk about ideas."

On the other hand, a sure way to destroy a relationship is for the man to refuse to discuss it. Women can put up with a lot, but if a man won't even discuss their relationship, it's all over.

This is, of course, the real reason Lady Chatterley ran off with Mellors. It wasn't that he was so great in bed, but the guy was terrific at discussing relationships:

Lady C: You really know how to please a woman, Mel.

Mellors: Wha'ya mean, luv?

Lady C: You say *all* the right things—"lasting commitment," "ongoing relationship." It drives me wild! What can I do for you?

Mellors: Nothin', luv. Want me t'talk dirty?

Lady C: I'd much rather you talked about *us.*

Mellors: Sure thing, luv. I never had a meaningful dialogue before wit' one of me women.

Lady C: Oooh! Say it *again.* I love it when you whisper in my ear about "maintaining our wholeness." You know how to say it just right. I just sorta tingle all over.

PERSONALS FOR THE RICH AND FAMOUS

A LAS, THE ADVENT of singles want ads came a little too late for some of the great all-time classified catches, both past and present:

Slim Self-reliant Woodsy Guy seeks similar self-sufficient woman for walks in the wilderness, long talks. Must have contemplative nature, ability to subsist on nature's bounty and love of outdoors, back packing, nuts and berries. P.O. Box 837, Walden Pond, Mass.

Single Jewish Femme, "guru-type," heavily into art and young writers, painters, et al., seeks avant-garde man (or woman) to share French literary salon. Love of Left Bank life, sidewalk cafés, vital. Cable: "roseroserose," c/o Shakespeare & Co., Paris.

Sports Legend, heroic proportions (Hall of Famer, ex-Yankee), aging gracefully, soft-spoken, silver-haired, seeks companionship in golden years. No sex bombs. Write "Mr. Coffee," Box 7580, San Francisco, Calif.

Aryan Dictator, upwardly mobile—average height, dark, mustachioed, with penetrating blue eyes—wonders if there's a blonde miss with good genes who's not afraid of a strong, dominant guy with a world vision. Loves pets, children, Wagner and military music. Box 1895, Munich, Germany.

Witty Irish Playwright, true esthete, poetic nature, impeccably turned out—seeks slim, graceful young man with delicate nature to share in life's bon mots. Call, *do not write*: O. Wilde, Box 6422, London.

Cloistered Poetess, virginal but willing to "try anything once," seeks tender soulmate for evenings by the fire, walks in the garden and chewing the fat. After sheltered life, am anxious to burn candle at both ends! Write: "Emily," RFD 9696, Amherst, Mass.

Older Man wants to satisfy satyric fantasies. Anything goes! Seeks partner—prefer Eurasian types—with literary and/or acrobatic bent. Whatever feels right. Contact: Mr. Miller, Big Sur, Calif.

Moody Misogynist Playwright, early 50's, looking for total woman without matrimony on the brain to explore delights of Sweden with no emasculating male-female hang-ups. Wire H. Strindberg, Box 652, Stockholm, Sweden, or call (800) 598–6470 (ask for Miss Julie).

Do You Promenade? Tat? English author, 40ish, proud but unprejudiced, seeks civilized gentleman for repressed relationship with faint romantic undertones. Reply: J. Austen, Hampshire, England.

Are You Man Enough For Me? Feminist leader, WJF, 50ish, slim and still a catch, no need for long-standing relationship. Wants guy for swapping views of public policy; informed, caring man who digs seminars. No one-nighters, please. "Gloria," Box 775, NYC.

Passionate Consumer Advocate, never married (tall, lanky, dark) wants similar selfless, dedicated woman also into uncovering corporate misdeeds and consumer rip-offs. Enclose photo with all moving violations in last two years. "Ralph," Box 8211, Washington, D.C. or (202) 555–0972 (pay phone, Dept. of Justice).

HERE'S TO THE LADIES AND GENTS WHO LUNCH

T HERE IS EVERY indication that lunch is becoming a more popular mating gound than dinner. Lunch is still a meal, while dinner is turning into grand opera.

Lunch in conveniently open-ended, custom-made for non-commitment. You needn't worry where to go afterward and can leave when necessary, for a variety of solid business reasons. Or you can stay put, if the magic is upon you, until they begin setting out the candles and dinner menus. Lunch beats drinks, which may ruin the night. About the worst that lunch can do is louse up the afternoon, which is largely downhill anyway.

You must decide, first of all, what sort of lunch this is—Relaxed, Romantic, Not Sure. It is fraught with possibilities (love has been know to break out over lunch), yet has less tension generally and carries fewer expectations, making it easier on all.

Most everyone is up for lunch, usually out and about, so there's less need for psychological primping, as at night. If it goes badly, you flee to your desk. If it goes well, you may never return. Lunch is light and merry. Dinner is an event, dark and ominous.

As lunch is a daylight event, presumably you are in basic control of your senses. It may also be a small awakening *(Hmmm, didn't notice that bald spot before . . . She seems a tad hippier than I recall).* Lunch has more reality to it; it's part of the day's rhythm, unlike dinner. Nothing too awful can happen over lunch—at least a first lunch; a second lunch is thinly disguised dinner. Bad stuff can happen at dinner, but most any dunce can make it through a tuna salad.

Though it still has a relaxed appearance, lunch is not what it was. Lunch has begun to take on certain dinner-like overtones. Lunch is now a sort of prelude—an audition for dinner.

You must choose the café carefully but with seeming nonchalance, on neutral ground. If you select too lavish a place, it could be intimidating. If it's too intimate, it could be misread. If it is too trendy, it's noisy and not at all, you know, *conducive.*

What you want, ideally, is a regular lunch spot (Le Café Conducive), as in old movies, where they know you ("Ah, Monsieur Rick, so good to see you again!"), though it may look like a calculated snow job.

Getting a good table is crucial to the future of a relationship. A "good" table involves a corner. A chronic inability to get good tables has led to the collapse of many couples ("Can't you just ask the maître d' for a better table? *I'll* do it").

To make the food appear secondary, you lightly brush aside the waiter a few times before finally settling on spinach salad and filet of sole. No matter what's on the menu, the woman invariably orders spinach salad. What did women eat at lunch in 1972, before the rise of spinach salad?

It takes a secure man to order spinach salad. A man by himself never orders spinach salad, but with a woman he'll order almost anything in hopes of appearing refined and sensitive.

What a man actually craves is a big cheeseburger, but when he's with someone he wants to impress he'll usually ask whether the fish is good so as to appear (1) in charge and (2) concerned about weight and muscle tone. Fish reveals you as a together guy who works out.

One thing you don't want to do at lunch is tear into the rye rolls, the way you do with friends. The toughest part of lunch with a woman is giving her as much attention as the rye rolls. Your really poised luncheon lothario totally ignores the rolls and butter, sipping a glass of wine . . . conducively.

The last hurdle is dessert and coffee. If things have gone well, dessert is an excuse to keep them burbling right along, though you have to be careful not to force unwanted raspberry torte down shy lunch dates.

If things are cozy, you can risk ordering something gooey with two forks (dessert is conducive as hell), but if it's still at zero, just the check, please. The American midday check-grabbing ritual has evolved into as delicate an art as the Japanese tea-serving ceremony:

Me: "Put that away! I've got it!" **She:** "No, no, I wouldn't hear of it. It's on me." **Me:** "But it was *my* idea." **She:** "No, this is my treat." **Me:** "Look, I've got my card out already!" **She:** "We'll go dutch." **Me:** "Don't be silly." **She:** "OK, it's my turn next time. Promise?"

This isn't male chauvinism. It's far worse—a sly ruse to encourage a second lunch.

GOD'S GIFT TO WOMEN (NO WARRANTY)

TONY D'PRINCE, the single world's leading perfectionist, met me for a drink at the Solo Lounge, where he spends much of his time in search of the perfect woman, who continues to elude him.

He couldn't wait to tell me of his latest disenchantment. "When I met Gina, I was sure I'd found my ideal woman," said Tony, ordering a spritzer, "only to discover she wears turquoise pantyhose. It's all over."

"It's good to see you haven't lessened your high, not to say narrow, standards," I said. "There's never been a woman in the Western Hemisphere—or world history—who could meet them. If you took out Aphrodite, you'd say she had stubby hands."

"Yeah, I once knew a gal like that," said Tony. "This Aphrodite, is she in advertising? I was gaga for Gina—until she showed up in striped turquoise stockings."

"Maybe your values are twisted," I suggested. "Does it matter if a woman happens to like colored hosiery? It's not like a major character flaw. She could be a loving person, with many fine compensating traits."

"She is. That's what makes it hard. Be honest, could you ever fully love someone with blue-green legs? Funny-colored socks reveal a trendy streak, deep down," said Tony, who, if he can't find a surface objection to a woman, will always uncover one underneath.

"Do you like Gina otherwise, socks aside?"

"I could accept turquoise stockings if it wasn't for her affinity for Neil Diamond. That just killed it."

"Perhaps, if you and she sat down, had a heart-to-heart talk and confronted the pantyhose and Neil Diamond issues head on, you could still work it out."

"It's too late," said Tony. "We went through color counseling. She won't stop wearing them for my sake. I respect her independence, but it's over."

"You're never happy. Remember Dawn, whom you dropped because she said 'martoonie,' 'veggy' and 'tennies'? And Lucy, who had a LOVE poster in her bedroom? You don't want a perfect woman. You want a paper doll you can remake each week to suit your ideal."

Tony grumbled, "I just don't want a woman who wears blue pantyhose to the opera having my babies."

"Does it make her less worthwhile, less feminine? What is it about 'veggies,' LOVE posters or multicolored stockings that prevents you from enjoying the full range of a woman's personality?"

Tony frowned, "I want someone normal, like me."

"You fall in and out of love for equally nebulous reasons," I noted. "You fall in love with concepts."

"What do you mean?" he said.

"Remember that woman you pursued halfway across the country because she had a certain way of tossing her hair when she laughed?" I asked. "Said it reminded you of Susan Saint James?"

"Oh, Sally?" he said, turning wistful. "Yeah, she had a terrific laugh, but it wasn't enough. She had a kid, too, and hummed while reading the paper." He made a face.

"I'd say you're doomed to remain single. You're just not willing to compromise, not even on the small things. How do you think you'll ever bend on the major issues that confront couples?"

"Laughing, legwear and humming *are* major issues," he said. "A laugh isn't everything—there's hair, eyes, legs—but it's not just physical stuff. There's also earning capacity, of course."

"Well at least you know what you want in a woman," I said. "A person who isn't into multicolored pantyhose or Neil Diamond and has long hands and a laugh like Susan Saint James."

"That sounds like the woman I'm taking out tonight," Tony said. "Her only problem is, she doesn't like me, which I find very hard to believe."

"Look," I insisted, "nobody's perfect."

"I know," he said. "I'm trying to be tolerant."

FANTASY UPDATE

AFTER READING reviews of Lonnie Barbach's collection of female fantasies, *Erotic Interludes*, I'm ashamed of how drab my fantasies look alongside those in her book.

Mine were never much to begin with, but in the light of recent disclosures by women about their fantasies, I see what a truly barren imagination I have.

It's disturbing to realize, in the erotica game, most women have got ideas that make me feel uncomfortable even being in the same room with a live female. God knows what's going on inside that teeming id.

Formerly, it was believed that men had the corner on sexual

fantasies, but, as in most things, the gals are making terrific strides and overtaking us. By 2000, they will have left us boys in the dust.

From all recent accounts, women have sexual ideas that make me want to hide under the bed. Most of their fantasies are well-

beyond anything I might conjure up. Many deal with parachutes or occur underwater—much too complex for your meat-and-potatoes sex fiend.

Even women's fantasy rejects would make my flimsy forays into the realm of sexual longing look skimpy, scarcely worthy of the word "erotic."

Knowing a bit about writing, I realize Lonnie Barbach has undoubtedly put the juicier stuff into print—orgies, latent lesbian desires, sex in space, one-legged lovers, filmed sex scenes— and left out the more humdrum frolics.

Even so, things are so bad in my imaginary sex life that I rarely have even routine escapades. The content of my sexual dreams would put Ann Landers to sleep.

Women I confess this to are polite about it and wink, "Oh, you just don't remember!" It's small consolation to know my mind is so apathetic that actual red-hot dreams can slip away as easily as all that.

All my erotic dreams deal primarily with the logistics of getting to the fantasy on time—parking, worrying whether I'm dressed properly, hunting for clean socks, losing the address, etc.

By the time the actual fantasy is about to commence, I wake up and have to begin all over next time; next time is always weeks away. It's a long time between dreams, even of the non-sexual variety, so I rarely get a full-fledged fantasy off the ground.

I prefer daydreams, which are easier to control, but even they're so humdrum I'm embarrassed to reveal them in public. They all occur on dry land, usually in a room, and never involve dwarfs, dairy products or metal appurtenances.

Male fantasies deal more in the general area of personnel, not so much with what as with whom. The what should take care of itself; I always figure I'll think of something.

From reading fantasies in sex magazines, I notice they tend to go into great detail, the area in which I am most deficient. At best, all I can summon up is a general idea; the setting is always hazy.

The details of my so-called fantasies (those in my dreams) are taken up with the difficulties encountered in arranging the tryst itself. It tends to occur either off-stage or at some later unspecified date. I miss all my own fantasies.

If I should awaken in a feverish lather, it never has to do with sex but because I'm in a strange neighborhood and can't find her house, or the car breaks down on the way, or I'm caught in a rainstorm.

I am sure these all mean something, but I don't like dreams that *mean* something; I want the graphic hard-core stuff without any footnotes.

In Ms. Barbach's book, there's a story about a woman warrior who sells a male sex slave into prostitution and another tale about a bisexual Buddhist who has a tryst with her lover in a temple as her husband stands by.

That's me over there, the one standing by, worrying what time the temple closes.

THAT OL'
BLACK BOOK MAGIC

THIS IS THE BIG week when I go through my address book with a jeweler's eye and decide who gets to stay in and who is finally, irrevocably, out of date. A ruthless process this, tossing people out in the cold.

"Address book" is a genteel euphemism for Little Black Book.

Little black books seem less blatant if they're green or blue. Mine is red, a gift from a gambling casino and worth at least $1.25.

I tried a *black* little book but it seemed too scheming; also too little. That's the first hard question to be addressed: Just how little should a little black book be? If it's too big and all-encompassing— if *any*body can get in—it loses its cachet. Should relatives be included? Doctors? Maids?

If it's too tiny, however, it doesn't really do the job, and you find yourself squeezing out people who, by all rights, deserve to be included. By people, of course, I refer to females, though recently I threw in a few men so it wouldn't look quite so sexist.

Which brings us to the nub of the issue: Who deserves to be in your little black book and when is it time to shake them out, a nasty chore that must be done periodically? It's like vacuuming between the sofa cushions—you never know who you'll find in there.

I'm too soft for the job. I let names linger long after they've moved on. When I cross out names, it feels like I'm bumping people off, which is why I delay as long as possible. There's always a chance I'll call someone I haven't seen since 1976. I've done sillier things.

Whenever I riffle the pages, I half expect new names will have written themselves in. Also, I keep certain names around for nostalgia's sake.

It should be a decisive split when I delete a name. Either the woman must have died or got married. I don't know anyone in jail, which might also require removal, but not necessarily. I bend the rules a lot.

Classically, of course, a little black book should include only viable members of the opposing sex. But life is complex, so certain questions persist, questions like: Should I excise a woman's name when she moves in with someone? Moves to L.A.? Is missing in action? Nowadays, almost anyone can get in there.

A year or so ago, the cross-outs began outnumbering the recent entries, so to make myself feel better I left in some names that, by any stretch of the imagination, should have been given the old heave-ho.

I have too many M's, so I'm taking a more hard-nosed attitude toward type-M women. It's also tough to make the book if your name starts with F or B, but I'm on the lookout for worthy H's, K's and Z's. It's next to impossible for an S to get in here; it would take a Streep or a Streisand.

I notice a few names of total strangers. Who, pray tell, is Helen Zekon? Marianne Farge? Anybody here named Joni Vincent? Will Patsy Decker and Sandy Heisler please go to the white courtesy telephone.

I have an informal three-phase screening process before anyone gets written into the book in ink. Getting into the book is tougher than getting out; it's like Stanford. Many a hastily scrawled name results in a lifetime appointment.

Step one is the Scrap of Paper phase, where names and numbers are scrawled on envelopes and cocktail napkins. These go under my office phone and, when that becomes a jungle, the names continue to phase two, my *office* address book.

This book is indeed black and includes virtually everyone—press agents, airlines, hotels, dentists, the city desk. It's no big deal to get in here, but it definitely beats being under the phone.

Phase Three is inclusion in the Little Red Book itself, though even this has a preliminary phase in which business cards and odd bits of paper are stuck under a plastic pocket in the back cover. This is like a trial period, lasting a few months.

Once a woman moves up from the rear pocket into the book proper, she's made the final cut and a champagne supper is held to celebrate the event. For those lucky names who survive this intense screening, all manner of nocturnal revels lie ahead. The rest is up to them.

HELLO FROM MY SCENE TO YOURS

Eᴀᴄʜ ʏᴇᴀʀ ᴀᴛ holiday time, I receive warm, bubbly letters from married friends, which make the unattached world feel pretty crummy.

Well, two can play at this subtle one-upmanship. Thus, in the spirit of these jolly seasonal reports, here is a letter from a single man to his married friends:

"Hello out there to all you residents of DomestiCity:

"Sorry I can't write everyone individually, but I've been too busy working the office party scene. This is always a busy season for me, the end of a chaotic yet *very* rewarding year (heh-heh-heh).

"**January** was a memorable month here at 572 Fast Lane, what with the new cat arriving. You can't believe how Taffy's grown! Cute as can be and, like her owner, smart as a whip. Won't be long now before she's ready to go outside. One day she's a helpless kitten and the next day she's all grown up and getting into trouble! What an animal. She's really helped me to mature.

"In **February,** my attentions turned outward. I had a major relationship for six weeks. Hope you didn't try to reach me here. I wasn't around a helluva lot. We were a pretty hot item. Carol says hello—or would, if I was still seeing her. Great woman: sharp, sensitive, adorable and great with animals. She and Taffy got along like old pals, but it wasn't meant to be. Some guy from her past turned up, so what can you do? Quite a month, all around!

"**March** found me at Sear's purchasing a new popcorn popper, with a unique butter-melting attachment, which pretty much occupied my time at the ol' VCR. I spent all my weekends taping classic *Saturday Night Live* shows but still found time for an occasional new film.

"In **April,** I began seeing someone at the office and did the rumors ever fly! A sweet person and we're still friends but Janet was too neurotic. Mood swings, tears, the whole bit. Who needs it, you know?

"In **May,** I fell in love and Valerie and I spent a great weekend in Calistoga that ended badly. It got too heavy. She's the clingy type and on the way back she was already talking about taking me home for Thanksgiving. It spooked me, but I learned a lot about myself, so it was a positive experience. No pain, no gain, as I tell the shrink. By mid May, I felt more centered.

"In **June,** I met a fabulous woman on the subway and, for a few days there, it looked like l-o-v-e. Delia claimed it was her punk look I fell for. We had some laughs. OK, she wasn't the classiest women I ever met but at this point in the year I wanted someone who wasn't into success.

"**July** was bleak, date-wise, but I welcomed a break. We've all been there, right? I needed to get back in touch with ME and was glad to spend quality time with Taffy, who craves more attention (those terrible twos!).

"**August**" was frantic, what with Nan flying in for a week and me breaking up with Carol and Valerie back in the picture. I also went into surgery and was laid off.

"**September** was real loose. Nan met some guy on the plane and Donna and I were at an impasse and Elaine went back to her husband, so I had more free time than expected and used it well to empty the wastebaskets.

"In **October,** I was a little down, so I called up a woman I used to date. Made me feel even worse. Taffy got a cold. I ate home twice."

"**November** found me knee-deep in desire. I met the woman across the street and we went to the zoo. This is IT! Helen likes her own space and yet has room in her life for me and Taffy. I am twice blessed!

"**December** was a time of gathering-in. Helen and I had some long talks and reached an understanding about exclusivity and 3 A.M. phone calls. It isn't perfect but we're working at it. Hope your year was as full of domestic uncertainty and romantic adventure as mine. That's it from here!"

A BRIEF HISTORY
OF NEW YEAR'S EVE

LIKE COCKTAIL PARTIES, singles bars and the Super Bowl, New Year's Eve exists in spite of the fact that everybody dreads it, or says they do.

From the moment you're old enough to date, New Year's Eve is a major worry. Before that, when you're a kid, the eve of December 31 is harmless, if sterile, fun, since no gifts are exchanged and there's nothing to eat. No animals get slaughtered, except on the highways.

It is ushered in quietly, with the sincere making of resolutions and the observing of people in Times Square going berserk, with cutaways to hotels where bulky people are pushing themselves across a dance floor and blowing horns in each other's face, and a grinning man in a blazer with shiny red lapels waves a baton.

This is New Year's Eve at its best, when you can watch the whole thing from afar and wonder about the mystique of adulthood and going out to celebrate and, the darkest mystery, all-night revels and kissing your favorite person at the stroke of midnight, a moment commemorated in song and story.

One year, when I was 14, I was considered old enough to accompany my parents to a true New Year's Eve party, the prospect of which thrilled me for weeks. I'd gone from pots and pans in pajamas to ginger ale at midnight.

At last, I would be privy to the secrets of night life on the greatest eve of the year. I would partake of group revelries indulged in by grownups, which gave me a certain apprehension. I was never really sure what my parents did when they ventured out in full-dress regalia.

All I knew was that, one New Year's Eve at our house, nothing happened except the telling of what I took to be dirty stories, overheard as I sat on a top step and listened to the muffled noise of knowing laughs, which had a different tone than daytime adult laughter, a little louder and longer.

Imagine my shock—and eventual delight—to learn that nothing outlandish went on in my parents' friends' houses. Not much drinking, none I was aware of, and a total lack of what might be called revelries. Most of the evening, in fact, was spent playing charades and twenty questions—for me, in those days, the pinnacle of sophisticated merry-making. It still seems the least lethal way to get through New Year's Eve.

Even at 14 you're aware this is a major occasion for those old enough to operate a four-wheel vehicle, whereupon it becomes the focus of your entire year, as you graduate to full-fledged grownup, entitled to all the attendant rights, privileges and sweaty palms.

One day you're a carefree 15.11-year-old, staying up late enough to go outside and set off firecrackers in the backyard (a clue to the dubious nature of the entire event) and the next year you're 16 and fraught with worry about seeing the new year in with a woman—one, moreover, you will be expected to kiss at midnight.

As if the occasion isn't awful enough on its own, it creates weeks of worry beforehand. In high school, it was necessary to begin cataloging prospective New Year's Eve dates in mid-November. As Christmas approaches, the night assumes milestone importance. You can't take just anybody. It was considered rude to ask someone for New Year's Eve without first taking her out at least once, for some trial kissing.

This meant you had to gear up by December 1st, allowing time for pre–December 31st dates before popping the question. There was added pressure to take not just anyone but somebody whom you could kiss with a certain ardor in front of others.

Those who went steady were forever pestering you, "Whyncha ask Cindy? Whyncha ask Gloria? Whyncha ask Joanne?"—to which my response was always, "Nah, I'm sure she's already got a date." This became self-fulfilling. If you waited long enough, they did have other plans, or said they did. Anything less than six weeks' notice was considered shamelessly gauche, an insult to her womanhood, if not all femalekind.

After a while, guys with dates began to badger you unmercifully. "C'mon, just ask someone. You can't stay home New Year's Eve." To stay home New Year's Eve was to be banished to some hideous colony peopled by drooling idiots and social defectives.

To ward off this fate, I found that the best defense against New Year's Eve was a good offense. For a time, I actually gave New Year's Eve parties, co-hosting them with a friend at his house, a large home with a "rec room" that boasted a bar where ersatz punch was prepared (7-UP with lime sherbet), crepe paper was hung and slow dancing was encouraged.

Since it was my party, I took charge of the music and made sure that the slow dancing began early, with heavy doses of Johnny Mathis, Joni James and Eddie Fisher. The Twist, the Bunny Hop, the Mambo and other unnatural acts were barred. Somehow, giving a party emboldened me to ask women who might otherwise be off-limits. One night a year I dated over my head.

Now, New Year's Eve is just another night out, only the traffic is worse and you conspire to avoid it. With luck, you escape into friends' homes where you tell risque stories while their kids sit on the top step and listen to the exciting sound of grownup laughter.